The Infertility

Copyright © 2021 by Kelly Maxine Bone

All rights reserved. No part of this book may be reproduced or used in any manner without written permission of the copyright owner except for the use of quotations in a book review. For more information,

address: kellymaxinebone@gmail.com

First paperback edition August 2021.

Get ready to laugh, cry and shout whilst reading The Infertility Diaries. I will take you on the long journey that we had to go through right until the very end.

I started this book as a blog, journaling everything I felt every time we went through something baby-related until we finally had our conclusion. Our road was long and sometimes hard but both the hubby and I got through it with love, perseverance and a lot of laughter. Now I know you're thinking how is infertility humorous? Well, quite frankly, it's not. But using my sense of humour, we got through some testing times with it.

Dedications

I dedicate this book to my awesome hubby and my amazing family and friends, especially my two besties, Laura Lund and Sarah Fryer, who have been through the tears, tantrums and laughter with me.

Most of all, I dedicate this book to our sperm donor, and London Womens Clinic Darlington, as without them our journey would not be possible.

Let's start at the very beginning

So, where do I start? Once upon a time? Here we begin? Or simply, this is us? I don't think it's really apt to use once upon a time because this is far from a fairy-tale, even though we're patiently waiting for our happily ever after.

But where did it all begin? First comes love, then comes marriage, then comes a big reality check and infertility! My story starts as far back as 2010, sitting in the doctor's office being told you have a condition called *polycystic ovary syndrome* and, at the young, immature age of 23, my reply was "and?" Looking back, I wish I had asked questions, wish I had investigated what I had just been told, not just shrugged it off as something inconvenient.

I mean, why at 23 would I even be thinking about having babies? Well, I wasn't as such. It all started when I didn't have a period for a full year and I had to wait the full year before the doctors would act. I gained weight like there was no tomorrow and I had random hairs sprouting from places no woman should have to endure, to the point where I was shaving everyday just to feel somewhat normal. At this point in my life, I wasn't in a particularly fulfilling relationship and I felt somewhat isolated from the world, but I plodded along for another

2 years until I could finally take no more and I had to escape from that toxicity.

Single and ready to mingle once more, I began dating until the point I got bored and stopped. Still, at this point, I wasn't thinking about babies or my PCOS (polycystic ovary syndrome) as I was only 25. I always knew I wanted to be a mammy but I just never had the right relationship, and I'll be damned if I was ever going to fetch a child into a toxic relationship; I would not be part of that all too well-known statistic.

So in 2013 I met my now-hubby, through a colleague at work. At this point I had completely sworn-off of men as I was concentrating on getting my life sorted - I'd just bought myself a house which I could finally call home - but I couldn't help being intrigued by him, so when he messaged me and asked me if he could buy me a coffee, at first I was hesitant. I knew he lived 2 hours away from me and I'd done long distance before and it hadn't worked - although perhaps it was slightly different as that guy had a secret family hidden from the world. So how did I know this was going to be any different? The difference was that the hubby travelled for work and was all over the UK, but he was mainly situated in Doncaster, which isn't that far away from me, and also he was willing to travel too so it wasn't all one sided. I had also done my digging to find that he didn't have some secret closet family too.

A few weeks, and a few dates later, the hubby dropped a bomb, and we're not talking farts here, he said to me, "Kelly, I've got something to tell you, and I completely understand if you don't want to go any further with the relationship. I'm infertile. I can never give you children". I remember saying back to him that that was okay because there's a good chance I would struggle to have kids because of my PCOS diagnosis (I'd finally got around to doing some research). Although, in the back of my mind, were all the questions of if's, and buts, and maybes.

I went home to me mam that night and opened up to her, asking her what I should do. She just simply said, "You need to think about this long and hard and is it something you can work through?" Then said the words, "Does he make you happy?" My mind was already made up at that point but you always need reassurance when it's something as big as this. Speaking to the hubby the next day, I said, "You being infertile won't put me off of you. If we have a strong relationship, we can simply work through this, and nowadays there's so many things doctors can do for us". That was that. Months went by and he moved into my house. Then, a few years went by and we bought our first house together and got engaged in the same year. 2 years after that we were married, and then a year after that, we were now officially trying to conceive with a little help from our donor friend.

So, that's my story, shortened because there aren't enough pages for the rest of it and I can fill you all in as the story goes along. Let's just say, life has never really been easy but then again whose life is? All I know is, if it wasn't for my friend's and family, I would've gone stark raving mad by now. Okay, well madder than I already am, as I am a teeny weeny bit bonkers!

The epically long journey started today

So today was our first official appointment. My hubby had booked our train tickets - first class, of course; we must travel in style on special occasions - it just must be done!

The excitement had started to settle in. I felt like I was travelling with a million butterflies in my belly! Were we going to have a baby by the end of the year? Eeek - words couldn't describe the feelings that we both had that morning.

First thing's first though, we had to meet up with the sister-in-law and our youngest nephew for some lunch and playtime at the Discovery Museum. A kids' play area where adults go free - now there's a new one. I don't know who had more fun playing with water and plastic boats, me or the nephew.

After a couple of hours of family time, we had to go to our appointment. I was full of giddiness but also that little bit of apprehension because this was something that was out of my control. Yes, I openly admit that I am 100% a control freak and I really don't care who knows - if you don't like it, tough; deal with it.

Anyway, we got to the Centre for Life and it wasn't what I was expecting. It had the feel of an office block rather than a hospital. Although it had that hospital smell (I don't even need to explain that - you know what I mean). We actually had to sign in as visitors. Seriously, who signs into a hospital? The nerves were settling in so much that I felt like I kept needing to go pee but daren't in case they needed me to pee during an examination. I then got called in for height and weight checks - why oh why did I wear jeans? I know they add 3lbs to me and Ugg boots, seriously, what was I thinking?!

Our names were finally called into an office-looking room and we weren't with the doctor that I was hoping we were going to be with. After doing all my research on her, we were stuck with another doctor and her student. Sigh.

The questions began:

How long have you been together? How long have you been trying for a baby? Have you got any medical conditions that we should be aware of? Why are you here today? What made you choose Centre for Life? The list was endless for both myself and hubby.

Just to answer a few of the questions as I live by the motto *shy bairns get nothing*. In other words, if you don't ask a question, you don't get an answer. At the time of the questions, me and my hubby had been together for 5 years and married for 4 months. We hadn't technically been trying to get pregnant because of the third question. We knew it was impossible, almost, not even a 1% chance. When I met my hubby, within 2 weeks he had told me that he had a condition called Klinefelter (xxy) Syndrome, which in turn had made him infertile. He had known since he was 17, but to add to that, when I was 23, I was diagnosed with polycystic ovarian syndrome, which hadn't caused me a lot of problems except irregular periods and weight gain, oh and the odd bit of random hair sprouting from places it shouldn't be sprouting from!

So, there we were, two people with random hormonal conditions; a car crash waiting to happen, or a match made in heaven? Luckily for us, it was a match made in heaven. I was never going to ditch this awesome guy just because 'biologically' he couldn't give me children.

This leads me on to the next question, "Why are you here today?" After many heart-to-heart conversations with the hubby, we had decided the best and really the only route we wanted to go down was by using donor sperm. It was that simple or so we thought.

The spanner in the works.

Yes, we could use donor sperm and yes, they would match my hubby's characteristics as much as they could but to even get to that stage was like we were horses in the Grand National, jumping over the many hurdles.

Hurdle number 1

I was too fat. Yes, ladies and gentlemen, apparently you can be too fat to have a baby now. Those damn jeans and Ugg boots. And it didn't help that my boobs weigh a good 9lbs either. The doc didn't even really beat around the bush with this one. Cutting the long story short, I would need to lose 4stone in 6 months. I mean seriously, I just need to sniff cake and I gain 10lbs!!

Hurdle number 2

To use donor sperm, you have to have a psych evaluation, which is fine, no problem at all. But, the way me and my hubby get through most things is with our humour, and I didn't think a psychiatrist was going to take too kindly with me telling her how he bought me a turkey baster as a Xmas present when we got our letter through. We might have to tone that down a bit.

Hurdle number 3

I suffered from chronic migraines and I was on very strong medication called Topiramate but, when I tried to come off it, it would send my hormones into overdrive and my periods just wouldn't happen or, if they did, I would think I was dying!! So, with all this happening, it would mean blood tests, which means needles - yack, yack, yack - I can't do needles. Nope. I won't do needles. They could take their needles and shove them where the sun doesn't shine!

Okay, so comparing it to the Grand National was maybe a bit melodramatic but that's just what it felt like. I left the hospital feeling like a big fat horse, and I was all optimistic going in. I left feeling like I just wanted to cry. But I wouldn't let this get the better of us. Our determination to have a child was strong and we were strong together but it just looked like tea is lettuce leaves from then on.

Big kids at heart

So after we got the news that I was a fat horse and would have to eat lettuce leaves for the rest of my fertile life, we decided to go for a break. And where better to go than Paris, the city of Love (think I've just been sick in my mouth writing that mush). Nope, we didn't go for love, we went for Disney - well fake Disney anyway - the *real* Disney will always be Disney World in Florida to me, where my hubby proposed. *Balk* That's enough of that mushy crap!

The thing is, spinning round and round on the teacups, giving yourself a headache and making yourself feel sick is all good fun, but we both couldn't help but feel like something was missing right slap bang in the middle of us. And looking around, and realising that we were actually the only adults on that ride, I think said it all for us. But heck, that was not going to stop us having fun. On to the carousel - gee up horsey. Round and round and round and there was me patting my horsey telling it to 'gee up'. I realised at that moment that, *when* we have children, they would be bonkers if they took after me. I was already known as the crazy auntie so it would only be right that I have that title as a mammy right?

Into the gift store. Now I love these places but my hubby, on the other hand, not so much. He prefers to sit outside on a bench and nap. When it's Disney, I'm like a big kid; I love it!! I've been brought up with Disney all my life. We even had a Disney-themed non-tacky wedding. These gift stores though, there's just something about them, they just call my name. Anyway, I was having a good rummage around, usually for bargains, and, out of the corner of my eye, there it was with this halo of light around it: the baby section. My head was saying, "No, don't do it to yourself. You know you'll buy something and you'll have to stare at it and you might be barren for the rest of your life", but my heart was saying, "Go on. Just one little look. They are just so little and oh so cute and what if, oh what if!"

You guessed it, I asked my hubby and, what did he say, being the typical laid-back fella he is, "just buy it if you like it." So, I walked away with a yellow and grey Dumbo Babygrow, thinking that if all else failed, the dog would look cute in it as I know he fits in 9-12 month clothes.

The highlights of the trip would have to be: reliving my childhood memories on the teacups and the horses and seeing Mickey Mouse! Have you ever laughed so much that you nearly peed your pants? That literally happened to me on holiday. You know when you're walking and not really watching what you're doing, dragging a suitcase, well I just missed dragging it through a huge pile of poop and, I mean, I was shocked at the size of it. The fact that that actually came out of a human. But, the laugh factor was, they had taken off their t-shirt to cover it up but it didn't quite cover it. Well, how do you explain that to someone in French? Google translate didn't even have the words.

My weight loss at this point: 0lbs. I told you, I sniff cake and I gain 10lbs. Somehow, I needed to pull my finger out.

My biological clock was ticking

April is my favourite month because it's the month I was born. I do feel sorry for my parents though; it must've been their month of torture having a daughter like me, mwah ha ha. Apparently, I didn't sleep through the night until I was 3 years old so I think I may have been cursed a lot back in the early years. I make up for it now though as I can sleep for England! I hope that, when we have children, they sleep. I don't know how my mam and dad survived - thank goodness for ear plugs!

My birthday this year was rather different. I don't usually like a fuss, but all my family came over in the morning and then my besties came over and little Jacky Boy - my best friend's little boy, who is one of the cutest little boys ever. You just have to love him, even if he did find the dog's poop scoop and ended up chasing us around the house with it!

My other friend had a surprise present lined up for me in the afternoon, a date with a medium. Now I can sometimes be slightly sceptical but I thought, "hey we'll give it a go". And oh my, did she tell me some things. She hadn't met me before and had no idea of my name or anything before I met her but she knew that I was thinking of writing this book. She knew that me and the hubby were going to have trouble conceiving and that it wasn't so much of a problem with me. And she then told me it would all work out in the end and we would have a little boy and a little girl. So I wrote this in here so if it does happen then I can look back and say "ooooooo look she was right" and if not, well then let's just leave it at that shall we.

At the end of a brilliant birthday, the hubby surprised me with a birthday cake. Not just any birthday cake, a minion fluffy unicorn birthday cake that I went crazy for! Yes, I'm still very much a child when it comes to crazy birthday shit like that!

April highs: even with birthday cake, I lost 1st 5lb, somehow. I managed to pull my finger out from somewhere.

April lows: another year older, my biological clock was ticking or so it may seem.

Heart to heart

May Day was spent catching up with my girls in the hot tub, with Mr Jacky Boy, of course, and Little Miss Phoebe - my besties' little ones, although Pheebs isn't so little anymore. So, after a good gossip, hearing about Sarah's love life and Laura's upcoming wedding, we decided to all jump in the hot tub, ducks and all, for good old selfie time! What I didn't realise, until after the photo, was that some of my house may be child proof but then, when you don't have kids, you don't think about putting certain 'things' away. So, what duck did Jacky Boy have in his hands? Yes, that is the Ann Summers ducky with a dick - luckily for us, Phoebe thought it was a foot! My, my, the innocence of a 7 year old is so lovely to hear but, my God, did we laugh!

The hubby also informed me that he had booked our First Class tickets to Newcastle for our next fertility appointment on the 25th June. Once again, it must be First Class because it would be a special occasion. Personally, I just think it's his excuse because he likes the fact you get free food. Well, I say free but, for the price of the bloody tickets, I think you actually pay for it somehow! Nothing's ever free these days or, if it is, there's always a catch!

I was slightly more scared this time as I only had 1 month to lose 2.5 stone. Holy crap. This was much more real now; I really needed a kick up my arse. My bestie used the swear word at me the other day and said we should join the - dare I say it - 'gym'. I couldn't think of anything worse.

The hubby, on the other hand, came up with an awesome idea. One which he was also involved in, and would probably now hate me for writing as his mam will read this. But yes, he told me the best way to lose weight and burn calories is to have some good old fashioned nookie. Well it wasn't like I was going to say no to that now was I? It wasn't until after the exercise routine had surmised and we laid there having a heart to heart, putting the world to right and all that jazz, we realised just how simple it was for some people to get pregnant. Like the hubby said, "They're already taking bets on when prince Harry and Meghan will be pregnant. Wouldn't it be nice if it was just that simple for us?" The truth was, yes, it would be nice if it was that simple but, like I said to him, the facts are it wasn't and neither was it his fault that he was born with his condition, nor was it mine that I was born with mine. Some people can't help the way they are. They can't change it. But with added help, we could get what we desire at the end of it and we both loved a challenge, so bring it on!

Cadbury's or Calories

So, we started the month of June with the beautiful wedding of one of my oldest friends, Sarah. In our house, she was known as 'train Sarah' as she worked with - you guessed it, trains! It was mine and the hubby's first wedding as hubby and wifey so it made us think of our day. A whole day and yet how quickly a wedding day is over in the flash of a camera!

After the wedding, the fun didn't stop there. Phoebe's hot tub party was fast approaching. Oh dear God, 8 year olds running around my back garden. What had I let myself in for? "Okay, calm down Kelly," I thought, "This will give you a taste of what's to come, when you have your own kids' parties to organise one day. Calm down. Bloody calm down."

I had 'pass the parcel' to wrap; prizes to sort out; the cake to bake again - and again, as it somehow got cremated; the gazebo to put up - cue "Daaaaaad I need a favour please?" 31 and I still ask my dad for favours; the grass to mow; the dog poop landmines to scoop; the house to clean (would 8 year olds even notice if I hadn't hoovered?)

The list was never ending, but you know what, to see seven happy and smiling 8 year olds running around the garden and getting up to mischief, it was worth it all and I'd do it all over again. Even if the hot tub looked like a garden centre, with the amount of grass floaters - well at least it's only grass. Thank Goodness birthdays are only once a year.

The heartfelt moment of the day was - well actually there were two; the first one was when Phoebe was late to her own party. Well, rather her mammy was running late, (as usual ha ha ha). Anyway, two of Phoebe's friends turned up and I said to them that I was Kelly, Phoebe's Mammy's friend. Well they looked at me with pure puzzlement on their faces before saying, "Phoebe told us you were her Auntie." How do you explain that one? Well yeah, kind of, it's a good job they got distracted with the dog! I wonder if it's a Yorkshire thing? I used to have to call my Mam's best friend 'Auntie Sue'; even now, to this day I still do!! It still made me melt a little bit inside - bless her!

The next squishy heart moment was about halfway through the party, Phoebe was asking me when we were going to do the games and the Piñata and then, out of the blue she said, "Kelly, are you going to have babies soon, because you'd make a really good mummy?" My reply was just "soon sweetie, soon." Then off she went back to play again.

My heart melted because you can't explain to an 8 year old what you're having to go through. All I know is that, when we finally did have a child, I knew who would be one of the first in the queue for squishy hugs.

Phoebe's quote of the day, something which I now will be using, was: "Auntie Kelly, how many Cadbury's have I burnt?" Showing me her new Fitbit and me scratching my head, "Cadbury's? Eh?? Oh, do you mean calories?" Well that was it I was in hysterics and so was her mam. So, from now on calories will be known as Cadbury's. Well technically, Cadbury's is chocolate and chocolate contains calories sooooooo.

Weight loss: 0 pounds. Although, I'd lost inches - Goddamn inches. The doctors don't want inches; they want pounds or kilograms. Arrrggh! I can't win. Although I shouldn't moan as I was down 2 dress sizes. It was only 10 more days until our next appointment to be told that I was still a whale and therefore couldn't possibly carry a child!

Is there such a thing as 'too fat to be fertile'?

So, here we were yet again, on our way back from another appointment that I felt was a waste of our time and effort.

The hubby was excited, not so much about the appointment (as we knew what to expect), but about the free food on the train. Have I told you before I have a train geek for a hubby, who just happens to like food like most men? Me, on the other hand, I was so nervous this time as I knew what was coming. Well, I thought I did.

The train journey

Newcastle bound, with our First Class tickets for the special occasion. FREE food trolleys coming around with muffins, fruit, drinks, crisps, hot beverages, cold beverages and ALCOHOL - man that was staring at me and saying *drink me*! I felt like Alice in Wonderland. I thought, "it's going to do one of two things: make me hurl, because of my nerves, or make me hurl because it's 11am in the morning and I'd not had any breakfast." Add in the fact that I was a lightweight so either way it wasn't going to be a good idea.

I decided to stick with my Starbucks Soya Caramel Macchiato, even though that wasn't really going down too well. I was also one of those weirdos who takes photos of food everywhere we go. God knows why I did but I just did.

After the boring train journey, I got asked "Pleeeeease can we go to the Discovery Museum before we go for our appointment?" Now, I'm sure he thinks I forget things but that's usually because I pretend I do. But not this time, I remembered the hubby saying there was a new LNER train outside the museum. So, guess why he wanted to visit? Of course, I obliged because I'm a loving, doting wife etc. Nah. I just wanted anything for a daft photo opportunity. It just had to be done!

The Centre for Life

So, here we were, walking to the office-looking building, collecting our visitors' badges from reception and approaching the lift for the 3rd floor and then it happened: the nervous stomach, Starbucks coffee and orange juice had just hit the danger zone, and I got that feeling that I was either going to be sick or I was going to poo. I know for some people it's too much information, but for heaven's sake we all do it - some of us more than others, especially when the IBS strikes! Luckily, this time I knew I could go as I wasn't having any tests done. It was a relief and that's all I'm saying.

Preparation on point

As I knew this meeting was in June, I was praying and hoping for nice weather. Why? Because last time it was so cold. I was so well wrapped up; I had all my 'heavy' clothes on, oh and Ugg boots. This time, however, it was 27°C and it was 'shorts weather'. A cotton vest top, the lightest-weighing clothes I could find, and it worked! And I did find out that our home weighing scales like to add 2 pounds to us... naughty scales. I felt like I'd won the lottery when she told me I'd lost an extra 2 pounds. My hard work and perseverance were showing but still my BMI was still too high - cue feeling like a whale again. So, I was congratulated on losing the weight, but - there's always that bloody but - but I knew it was coming. "I'm sorry Mrs Bone but until your BMI is below 30, we can't do anything for you".

So basically, I was still too fat to have a child. But then, here was my big 'but', we found a clinic that takes patients with a BMI of 35 and who have had fantastic outcomes. So what next?

Too fat, yet I'm fertile

My BMI was too high. Okay, I got that. I knew that was coming before we went to the appointment. What I didn't expect was the doctor to throw another positive our way, mixed with a negative; it was a giant head f**k (sorry mam, I know I swore but I blurred it out for you, don't fancy a thick ear and all). "Well your BMI is too high but, from your blood tests, you're definitely fertile and ovulating fine so we don't see a problem with you conceiving. BUT just not until your BMI is below 30." Yes, I think I get it; my BMI must be under bloody 30 for God's sake! So technically, if there was no problem with my hubby, we could have had a baby together with no bother. So why was there so much pressure to lose weight? Was there such a thing as fatism?

I'm not usually a drinker but I felt like I needed one after that.

Home or hospital?

The turkey baster inspiration

This is where I get to talk about my favourite topic. The turkey baster method - ha ha! Yes, we had gone down the alley of discussing 'shall we/shan't we' and we'd concluded why not? It was worth a try wasn't it?! By the way, we just nicknamed it 'the turkey baster method' for comedy purposes and under no circumstances was I going to be putting any turkey basters near any fanjitas!

What is the turkey baster method?

In a nutshell, it's artificial insemination. Only, our version of the turkey baster method came to light after our last meeting in Newcastle. After finding out that I was highly fertile and getting pregnant wasn't going to be a problem, we figured out our only issue was, yet again, that we didn't have any sperm. It's not like you can pop down to your local Tesco and find it in their freezer section now is it?!

That's why it was going to cost us a fortune. But, here's the big 'but': there is a website on which people can donate sperm and even co-parent if that's something you're wanting. Amazing right? The trouble is, how do you trust a website? How do you know if these people are genuine? Because if it's for free, there's got to be a catch right? It turns out I was wrong. Yes, there is the odd moron on there but otherwise these men just want to help childless couples achieve their dream. They don't want anything out of it. The satisfaction of giving a human life is enough for them as most of them have families and don't want anymore children themselves or just generally don't want to have children of their own.

Using this information, we could pick the right person ourselves, matching hair, eye, skin tone and even blood group. So, there it was, all we would need to do is get the "express delivery service" and insert at ovulation and that's what the hospital was going to be doing for £3000. Yes, I know that the hospital would be doing a bit more than that but was it £3000 worth? Extortion at its finest.

Medication time, medication time, medication time. Before we could go down that route, I needed to come off my migraine medication again. It was damn hard last time but I think I needed to just persevere as I knew it will be worth it in the end. Also, I needed to start on the prenatal vitamins to get them into my system. Think me and the hubby needed to go shopping too. We needed to get supplies for our turkey baster trial method. Roll on 2019. Hopefully it would be our year.

A question with a thousand answers

The original recipe for a family:

- One loving man.
- One loving woman.
- One marriage and a perfect home.

Original Method

Married man and woman have sex in their perfect home and 9 months later a baby is born.

So that's what's supposed to happen in all the fairy tales, movies and books I've ever watched or read so why do they not show how it sometimes really happens? Why should you be ashamed of what's happening to you? After all, it's more common than you think. People just don't talk about it and you don't see it. Regardless of whether it's IVF, IUI, or the turkey baster method. That's the problem with society today. We are made to believe something that just isn't true so, when something like this does happen to us, it's like we've brought a great big ball of shame down onto our families.

Seriously though, I'm proud of what me and the hubby have gone through. Yes it comes with ups and downs but in turn it's made us stronger; it's made us talk to one another more so than ever before, after all, you are going through this as a couple, not alone like some people think they are. Your partners are going through this with you and want to be part of it too. Talk to them. Go on, what harm can it do? I don't know where I'd be without the support of my hubby. Oh yeah, I do, in a dark hole somewhere with a million and one questions in my head and wondering what he was thinking!

Stereotypical people problems

We get this one a lot. We've got the house and we got married so when were we going to have a baby? What were we waiting for?

First things first, just because we got married doesn't mean that we are going to be at it like bunny rabbits and popping out babies left, right and centre. Secondly, now here's the big one: what if we didn't want children? Obviously we did, but some people choose not to for their own reasons. Thirdly, what if we CAN'T have children because one or both of us are infertile?

In our case, I would simply turn around and say we can't have kids, not through lack of trying though. I did love to see people's reactions. After all, they did ask me the question in the first place and it would be rude not to answer and my mammy taught me not to tell lies! Also, I didn't feel embarrassed about what was going on because to me it was natural; it was our fairy tale. It *would* be our happily ever after.

This leads me onto the title of 'stereotypical people'; just because people get married, doesn't mean they have to have children. So guys, give all us newlyweds or happy couples a break. Please stop asking THAT question as you might not get the answer you were hoping for! And to everyone reading this who is in our situation, don't be ashamed of your unique story. Run with it. Don't bottle it all up to yourselves. Now, I'm not saying share it with every Tom, Dick and Harry but people need to become more aware of what they are asking because one question can open a lot of heartache. But sharing your experience can also half yours.

#Girls holiday

The holiday had finally arrived and I couldn't be anymore excited. After me and my bestie Sarah stayed in a hotel the night before playing giant Connect 4; I won, much to her dismay! My best friend, Laura, who was getting married later in the year was having her hen weekend with 11 of us. Originally, if all had gone to plan with our fertility journey, I should've been pregnant right then but things never go the way they are expected so I'd just have to wait a little bit longer. With me only needing to lose half a stone for our dream to come true, and the food being pretty damn crap in the hotel we were camped out in, I was optimistic that the scales wouldn't be calling me a fatty when I finally got home.

The hotel

Where do I start with this one? Fawlty Towers springs to mind. And The Inbetweeners Movie (on sight of the bidet) - only we didn't do a poo on the floor. We made the room sparkle from glitter and glamour night. We had to rent room fans, fridges, TV remotes - I mean come on you put a TV in our room but we had to pay for the remote? Well that was just rude! Not that you want to be watching TV anyway, but it's the principle. The food, as I said in the beginning, was what I like to call "samey". The same foods every day which tasted of either salt or sugar. The best meal I had was the McDonald's in the airport on the way home. The pool was like sardines in a tin. Now I love kids, obviously, but why is it that on holiday all they do is scream and splash and take over the goddamn big people pool? Bugger off into your own pool! As I was writing this, on my way home on the plane, I could see yet more glitter.

Homesick

I've always gone away and never been homesick but this time the homesickness settled in almost straight away. Maybe because I didn't have my cup of Yorkshire tea in my favourite Starbucks mug? But deep down, whilst all the others were telling me they were missing their kids, I was missing my dog! He was my baby, always had been, ever since I got him. Whilst I was away, it was his birthday and the hubby got him to open his birthday present and card and filmed it for me to watch and I couldn't be prouder. If I was like that with an animal, then what the hell was I going to be like with my own child?

The holiday overall was fabulous but I learnt that I was very much old before my time and I liked my home comforts too much. My God. I could murder a decent cup of Yorkshire tea - none of this Tetley or PG. shits. I used to be the soul of the party, the loud gobby one, but now I think I was more reserved, somewhat quiet, almost borderline boring and I didn't ever think I'd call myself boring.

No more shake, rattle and roll

In another episode from the day in the life of Kelly, I finally had the motivation to come off all my medication, which of course I knew I had to do, but I'd tried it twice already and failed epically. So, when I was writing this, I'd been off all medications for 3 weeks and I felt absolutely amazing.

Unfortunately, I was hungry all the time which, when you're trying to lose weight, really defeats the object. The scales were flicking to 2lb on and 2lb off. It was annoying the hell out of me. I was thinking, "Just stay off. I really don't want you, so go, just go and don't come back." Yes, Kelly, like fat is really going to listen to you yelling at it. I needed to get some motivation to lose some more weight so I started looking back at pictures from when I felt like a whale in comparison. I couldn't believe how far I'd come but I still had a long way to go.

I know that some of you will think that it's easy to just stop stuffing your face but, the thing is, I was never like that. Yes, I could eat but I didn't over engorge. My trouble was that I didn't exercise. It was partially down to not liking the - cue the swear word - gym. I could walk, but if you don't work up a sweat there's really no point, and the book of excuses started all over again. My favourite excuse was that "I've had a long day at work and I just can't be arsed". I know that type of attitude gets you nowhere but how do you change it when it's all you've ever known? Well - newsflash - if you want to have a baby, you will have to lose weight. That means eating right and doing exercise. Even the hubby ended up on the road to losing weight and looking amazing, not that he needed to because I love him no matter what! The relief of not shaking, rattling and rolling anymore was fabulous and I'm glad I finally got the motivation to come off my meds.

The first medication I had to combat was my head meds - Sertraline. I was put on these after I was diagnosed with PTSD following a trauma that occured 3 years prior. But since having counselling, I realised that I wasn't going stark raving mad. I had my issues. I needed to let them go and deal with it. The medication was just a crutch and I hadn't looked back since coming off them. I felt somewhat normal now.

The next medication was Topiramate. I was put on this for chronic migraines and it had been a Godsend but I found out that, if I fell pregnant on it, it could deform the foetus. This medication was hard to come off. I'd tried twice already and failed but this time I had determination on my side and tiger balm, lots of tiger balm (it's an amazing natural migraine relief). What I didn't know about this medication until I came off it was it is also an appetite suppressant which was why I felt hungry all the time. Since coming off it too, we'd had thunderstorms, which is my BIG trigger and I only ended up having a very mild migraine, whereas before I would've been bedridden. All in all, determination really is the key to success.

How to borrow a child

Ingredients:

- Take one stressed out parent in the school holidays
- Take one 8 year old little girl

Method:

Ask said parent if you can take said child out for the evening and have a sleepover. Wait 3 seconds for a look of sheer relief on said parent's face. Wait 2 more seconds for the obvious answer of "yes". Take her and go, go, go.

Me and the hubby borrowed my friend's little girl, Phoebe, for the night. There was a method in my madness of borrowing a child, as Incredibles 2 had just been released and, as it was a kids' film, we didn't want to be the only childless adults in the cinema. The only problem with that was that Pheebs had already seen it so we went bowling instead. The first stop was Pizza Hut; we needed that little subsidence for bowling if I was going to win, of course. Only, little did I know, after teaching Phoebe how to bowl without the ramp, she would kick my butt!

After much fun in the bowling alley, we headed to Starbucks for coffee, or hot chocolate or even tea but nope, this child wanted water. I mean, I'd never say anything to anyone who's trying to be healthy but who goes to Starbucks and just drinks water? That's like me going to a steakhouse and ordering tofu! Crazy child! We did have a few chuckles when she won some fart putty, of all the things she could've chosen, yep, you know it, she went for the most gruesome thing they had to offer and was of course sat making it fart, followed by the words "excuse me!" I hadn't laughed like that in such a long time.

Home time was quick and easy: pyjamas, squishy hugs and then bed - to sleep like a log - as we all had a big day the next day: Flamingo Land.

The next day

The 9 o'clock pick up for Laura and Sir Jacky Boy didn't quite go to plan as I was late - as always. I'm one of those people who would be late to their own funeral. We got there eventually and then we were off - whoop whoop. Note to self: don't buy crayons to keep the kids quiet because a 2 year old thinks they are yummy for his tummy. On a plus note, the colouring books made great wasp swatters as Flamingo Land was rife with them.

We all had an amazing day there going on rides, playing in water, eating ice-cream and Jack finding dinosaurs and shouting "roar" to the entire park. What I learnt from my experience of borrowing a child and entertaining two of them at Flamingo Land - well maybe three of them if we include Laura, was that I am an awesome auntie! I also learnt that, even for such a short journey, kids make an almighty mess in the car. But, all in all, these two kids are amazing and I am very grateful to be in their lives.

Friends' day out

You know when you take your best friend out for the day and it feels like taking a 3 year old out? "Oww my feet hurt. I don't want to carry the bags. I need a drink. I need food. My back hurts. My head hurts. I'm thirsty. I feel dizzy. I'm tired." But God do I love her!

I had the most amazing day out in Manchester with my bestie. I took her on a surprise outing; well, it would've been a surprise if the taxi man hadn't said, "Oh, are you going on the Coronation Street tour?" Why else would I have given you that address in secret? At least Sarah was surprised as she had no idea where she was going - hence why she'd worn heels. I probably should've thought that one through; cobbled streets and high heels don't really mix do they? Probably should've told her to wear trainers specifically rather than telling her the dress code was smart casual.

So, at the end of the tour, her feet were starting to ache and we still had 5 hours until we had to catch the train home. Of course this meant shopping time. Primark. Oh my days, the shop I love and loathe all at the same time. I don't understand how anyone could spend over an hour looking at the same clothes that was until I took Sarah in there. So many knickers. Seriously, how many types of knickers can a girl wear? You've got mini, midi, Brazilian, thong, full, high leg and the list goes on. All that men have is either boxers or y-fronts. Lucky for the men is all I'm saying!

After a bit of shopping, and starting to feel a little bit hangry - yes, that is now a word - we found a nice little Italian for lunch. Although I did think Sarah was a little shocked at the size of her pizza; it was the biggest I'd seen! I couldn't actually believe that she managed to polish it all off. Where on earth did she put it?

We then had 2 hours to get the rest of the shopping done and catch the train, so we cracked on. The hubby needed new vests for our upcoming holiday so into Next we went. Too late though, all the winter stuff was in and all the summer clothes had gone. Did people not vacation at any time of the year anymore?

Upon leaving Next, we had to go down an escalator, which was where I got to laugh my socks off: I went first, leaving Sarah at the top. At first, I couldn't understand what she was doing until she shouted, "it's too fast". How is an escalator too fast you ask? Well, when you have a suitcase, high heels and no balance, it's too fast. It was a good job that a lovely kind mister helped her down or I think she'd still be there now.

With only 1 hour left until we needed to be homebound, you guessed it, we weren't going to make our train because somebody's feet were now starting to ache and swell. Happy days that Shoe Zone was in the Arndale Centre. Unfortunately, this was Sarah that we were talking about. It wasn't going to be an easy mission. Nope, they had to look pretty and go with the outfit and be comfortable all in one go. In the end, she settled on slippers - yes, pink fluffy slippers.

There was one last stop before the station. I was in desperate need of a jumpsuit - something comfy to sit on an 8 hour flight with. Unfortunately, having big boobs and finding something to fit Bill and Ben in was much harder because all the clothes shops make clothes for girls with small boobs. It was like I was a minority as I have boobs, although I knew I wasn't! After trying on 8 jumpsuits, and struggling to fit the twins in any of them, I gave up.

Then we realised the time! Shit! There was only 15 minutes to get to the station for our train. "Taxi!" Only, the taxi driver dropped us at the wrong end of the station, and every traffic light was against us. 4 minutes to walk to the other side of the station, and through what seemed like a maze of a carpark, we made it, only to see our train pulling away.

As I'd bought advance tickets, I knew we would have to pay extra so I thought I'd try my luck and charm and get the fee waived. Told our story of how we missed the train to a lovely dispatch lady, Netty, and she helped us get on the next train. I could've literally hugged her but I restrained myself. Instead, me and Sarah treated ourselves to a Starbucks - which helped take the edge off a little. I would've preferred a glass of wine, but coffee had to do.

Before we got on the train, I was asked a rather bizarre question: "Kelly, if I died what would you miss most?" It was the easiest question I'd been asked all day. "Everything, Sarah, you come as a package and there's not just one thing I'll miss most. I'll miss everything!" I meant every word of it. The phrase 'you can pick your friends but you can't pick your family' sprung to mind. "Sarah, you are part of my family and my life would be incomplete without you in it. My sister from another mister. Love you girl!"

Love was in the air

Love had been very much in the air. The hubby and I celebrated our first anniversary and my bestie married her Prince Charming.

Me and my hubby met on the 18th February 2013 in a little signal box called Saltmarshe, where I used to work as a signaller, and he worked on the tracks. Unfortunately, it was getting knocked down and I was upset that we wouldn't be able to show our future children where we met. So, as a sneaky surprise, I decided to organise a photoshoot in our wedding attire. Any excuse to get in my wedding dress again.

I'd led the hubby to believe we were going to York Races with my bestie Sarah and her friend and, on the day, which was the day before our anniversary, I was able to get my hair done and get him in a suit without him getting suspicious. Sarah arrived at 10am, decked out in her race attire, because we had to keep up the charade until just before we left. The car was loaded with all our wedding bits, including the brollys that we wanted to use as props. So after a few last-minute bits, we were on our way. But not before I blindfolded the hubby though, to totally throw him off the scent.

We arrived to my parents waiting for us - ready with camera in tow - because my dad had volunteered to do the photography for us. The hubby stepped out of the car, took the blindfold off, and, after a few choice words and a moan about my rather bad driving - well, he isn't wrong there, I am a typical female driver - we began. He loved his surprise and definitely had no idea where we were going. Well done me for keeping the secret.

We went up to the box for a quick change into THE dress. But as I'd lost weight, it needed some serious pulling in and I'm glad that was Sarah's job. After the shoot, me and the hubby headed to yet another surprise that I had set out; we were staying overnight at the Grand Hotel and Spa in York. This also had history for us too: I lost my first engagement ring - or rather, it was stolen from a hotel room in Newcastle - so the hubby had secretly bought me a new ring and re-proposed to me at the Grand Hotel in York at the end of 2015. He'd wanted the ring to have meaning too - the big mush!

What I didn't expect, however, was that the hubby also had a surprise for me. Two tickets to visit New York at Xmas. This was on my bucket list so I was over the moon! We had always said that we wanted to do this before we had babies, but I never expected us to be able to complete our mission. We hoped that the New York break would be the last one as just the two of us!

The wedding of the year

My bestie was getting married!

September arrived, with the excitement of my bestie, Laura's, wedding! I just love weddings; they are so happy and joyful and exciting all in one! Even more so when it's your best mate marrying her "babe". (Yes, Laura I cringed writing that word!)

The day started with us all piling in at Laura's mam's house to get our hair and make up done. And shit loads of glitter was sprayed into our hair courtesy of moi! I'd already done my make up before I got there, because nobody touches this face. Nobody! I was so fussy when it came to make up; I needed my Estée Lauder double-wear trowelled on my face! I did however have the job of doing the mini maids makeup, which they sat so nicely for. That was until they saw the unicorn face powder and face mist and went crazy for it. I don't blame them really as I did the same thing when I bought it. 'Gimme the crazy unicorn shit!'

Then it was bacon butty and brew time for everyone, including the bride. It had to be done; you can't get married on an empty stomach!

The morning passed so quickly and all was calm and relaxed; the calm before the rain! We all got into our dresses and then it was time for the bride to get into hers.

Seriously girls, don't use stick-on bras, what a palaver they were; they stuck to everything except your boob!

We got into the cars and headed straight into Selby Abbey. Did I mention it was raining? Not that that would spoil their day; it just meant we got a little, shall we say, damp. The ceremony was short and sweet and I only got emotional twice: once when Jacky Boy first saw his mammy and his face just lit up; and the second, when Laura got to the end of the aisle. The tears were coming but I sucked it up because nobody wants to see a crying face in their photos! The vows were done and my bestie is now married to babe. It only felt like 5 mins ago when she told me she was getting engaged and then, all of a sudden, it was done.

It was time to get out in the rain, do some quick photos and jump in the car to the P.A.R.T.Y. At the wedding breakfast, I had the sheer pleasure of sitting next to Sir Jacky Boy, who, may I add, was not only as good as gold, but he looked ever so cute in his little suit. We sat eating our food, watching Dinosaurs and shouting "roar" whenever we saw one - that was definitely a must! After a lovely meal and countless "roars", it was on to some good old-fashioned drunk dancing. I'm not sure what it is, but when I'm slightly drunk, I think I can really dance. *Newsflash Kelly you really can't!* I was, however, impressed with myself that I stayed in high heels all day long.

All in all, it was the best day of the year so far. All the planning for the big day to be over in a flash of a camera but the memories will live with them for the rest of their lives.

It's all about the egg whites

When you're trying for a baby normally or our way, it's all about peeing on sticks, testing body temperature, and checking out cervical mucus (TMI I know). But it's all about the egg whites honey - and we're not talking about food! Oh, and don't forget the prenatal vitamins everyday. You become somewhat obsessive with ovulation calendars and period trackers and, when you've got PCOS (polycystic ovary syndrome), it makes it twice as hard because mine would change monthly! Don't even think about long haul flights as that also changes your cycle. Oh my days! Why could nothing ever be simple?!

So, us women have our period and then, a week after it has stopped, we begin the routine of peeing on a stick daily and nightly because that's what Google and the doctors tell us to do. What does Google know? Well, apart from everything!

Don't even get me started on the apps. There's no app for someone with PCOS. I mean, I'd ovulated twice in one month according to the app and pee sticks combined. So, either I'm superhuman or there's a fault in said app! There I was waiting for Mr Blobby to arrive - yes, my period has a nickname; I found Aunt Flo somewhat boring. And then the routine would begin all over again.

The trials and tribulations of the spunk run

Contracts were signed. Here we were - officially trying to get pregnant, using the artificial insemination aka turkey baster method. I had so many people ask me questions about what we were doing because people found it 'weird'. But, then again, what was 'normal' in this day and age?

Here's the explanation to it all - in graphic detail (you've been warned). I must reiterate, even though we call it the turkey baster method, no turkey basters were actually involved in this process - although it's rather funny to imagine and would've been a great story to tell the child when they get older.

The turkey baster involved in our method was a sterile 5ml syringe and the hubby's sperm was replaced with our amazing, generous anonymous donor, who shall not be named. But, just to add into this part, they offered to help us and I don't think they quite understood how big of a deal it actually was for us. That this one person would try to help us change our lives forever. Not only that, but they were willing to do it, not because they feel sorry for us, but to quote what they had said "That we would make amazing parents and they have no doubt about that and that we actually deserve it". How do you thank someone for doing something like this for you? The truth is, no matter what we do, it will never be enough to show how grateful we are to he who shall not be named. They are the light and hope in our dark dismal tunnel and proof that there are some genuine people left in the world.

I used OPK's (ovulation prediction kits) so I knew when I had ovulated. Not only that, but I always get, what I can only explain as, a 'pop' feeling in whichever ovary has released the egg and the egg white cervical mucus, which I explained in my last post.

We weren't going to start the whole process until December as we had two holidays coming up and I didn't want to fly if we managed to conceive. Only it didn't quite work out that way. On the day I ovulated, my hubby announced it on the group text and asked if our donor was free. It was an 'if he is, he is' scenario and, luckily for us, he was. So that was it, our minds were made up. It was happening faster than I anticipated. What an exciting and emotional time, full of hope and optimism, but with that slight fear of 'oh my f*****g God this is actually happening'. Even though in the back of my head I had that nag of 'it's probably not going to happen'. This would be our 'trial run', to see how we're all going to do this thing.

On the first time it happened, the donor dropped his 'donation' off at our house and then we proceeded to use our method of warming it up until it liquidised, followed by, using the syringe, and inserting it as close to my cervix as possible, with the added benefit of preseed (a natural lubricant). I had this recommended to me because it doesn't kill sperm off like some lubes and it can actually help in making the little swimmers find their way to the right place. After laying with my butt in the air for 30 mins, the process was complete for that day. It was as easy as 1,2,3.

One round down, one more to go. So, the second round was slightly different to the first. I was working a 12 hour day shift and couldn't expect the donor to always come to ours so I asked if I could pick up the 'donation' after work, which he was more than willing to help with. The only issue I had there was the timing. I had to get there, get the pot and get home within an hour of the 'donation' being distributed - easy right? Wrong. As the 'donation' must be kept at body temperature, and I had to drive home and couldn't heat it within my hands, I had to use my cleavage. At least they come in handy for something, even if it was only to keep the 'donation' warm. I nicknamed this run the 'trials and tribulations of the spunk run' because the damn pot lid kept popping off as I was driving. I really didn't want a car covered in the little swimmers so I kept having to drive and rearrange.

Finally, home was on the horizon and I couldn't have been happier. At least with the donation being kept in a warm booby environment, it had liquidised so it was easy to do and there was no waiting this time. In it went. Now it was time for the dreaded two week wait.

Let the two weeks wait commence

Trying to conceive key:

TTC - *trying to conceive*

CM - *cervical mucus*

DPO - *days past ovulation*

AF - *Aunt Flo*

AI - *artificial insemination*

PCOS - *polycystic ovary syndrome*

The Witch, Mr Blobby and, sometimes, **'she'** - *period*

So here it was, the start of our two week wait. I say it was ours because the hubby was just as excited as me and was having to listen to me moan everyday!

And so, it began. I ovulated on the 13th of November, according to every pee stick I used and had accounted for. We did the artificial insemination on the 10th and the 11th; the sticks have a clear indication on these days too and, according to Google, sperm can live in one's warm vagina for a few days.

So, 1 to 2 DPO I felt nothing - but that's normal right? Then we moved onto 3 DPO and we were going on a weekend break to Berlin, which was only a short flight, so I wasn't worried. I remember I had serious amounts of

CM, which I thought "Oh here we go, Mr Blobby is on its way, typical when we're away."

4 DPO: this is the day my normal period was supposed to arrive but nope she didn't show. Instead, I was left with, all I can explain is, a feeling of blood rushing through my body and heading straight for my clit - yeah, you got that one wrong didn't you? You expected 'genitals' or some other nice word for it but Kelly doesn't beat around the bush with words!

So, here I was, in the middle of Berlin, telling the hubby that we needed to go back to the hotel NOW. This was far from normal for me because, over the last couple of years, my sex drive had somewhat diminished. Not that he complained either way.

Only, nothing seemed to satisfy that 'feeling'. It was like my clit had just woken up and gone 'hello world!' The hubby was also delighted to keep reminding me how much I was going to the toilet as well. I just kept telling him it was 'because the cold hit me and I needed a wee' or that 'I had a bladder of a 2 year old'. At that point, I was secretly thinking that Mr Blobby was going to show up any second because I always need to pee more and kept having copious amounts of CM (nice right?). Not!

5 DPO: we were on our way home from an amazing weekend away but not before I had to have an afternoon nap as I was so tired. I was still peeing constantly and my boobs had started to hurt. So, to me, that definitely

meant that Mr Blobby was imminent - only she didn't show her ugly head.

6-7 DPO: I caved and peed on a stick. Of course it was going to be negative; what the hell was I thinking? Goddamn my impatience!

I also realised that, after 10 days and thinking that I was now 10 DPO, I realised I had miscalculated and was only 7 DPO. More waiting! I had been calculating from the day we had actually inseminated, rather than the ovulation which was 3 days later! Could I have been any more frustrated? To top it off, I dropped a yoghurt that I had just bought and had a complete meltdown, crying because I'd dropped it and then angry because the dog didn't like banana flavour yoghurt, which meant that I'd actually had to clean it up. Upon cleaning it and chuntering to myself, I then managed to get my foot stuck in a bag. Well that was it. I lost it and decided that 'f**k the world' was my phrase for that day! I needed sleep.

8 DPO: I woke up with what I would describe as really bad period pain and thought well that's it we're out this month. But no, my body was evil and she still didn't rear her ugly head. Nothing. Not even a speck. What was going on? Seriously, I couldn't take much more. I felt like the two week wait could kiss my arse! I was still tired all day. I was still slightly crampy but it was no longer painful and my boobs felt like giant rocks. Oh,

and my sex drive was still through the roof, even with a headache; lucky hubby is all I'm saying!

9 DPO: Still negative - not that I expected anything different. There was still no sign of the Wicked Witch and she was now 5 days late. Because of my PCOS, she could arrive at any time. Although I had been regular, almost like clockwork, for the last 6 months so why was it now that she decided to play mind games with me?

I had woken up that morning to the smell of puke. It was that bad that I nearly puked at the smell. Thanks Monty. That's really what I wanted to wake up to, your pile of sick on my bed. I was still tired all day and peeing constantly. I had AF-type mild cramping (this was confusing to me as I would usually only get cramps on the 2nd day into my period). I cried at the telly during the morning because someone got sent home from MasterChef. I seriously felt like telling myself to pull myself together. There were serious amounts of CM too. So much so that you could spread it on goddamn toast! #masterchefgoals

10 DPO: Yet another day, yet another symptom. I almost got to that point where I felt like I was actually waiting for my period to start. I needed to try and resist the temptation to test until Monday as this was when my 2 week wait would officially be up. Until then, it was just a waiting game and I just had to keep telling myself that 'either way it's going to be ok'. Even if Mr Blobby

arrived, we would just start the process all over again and if it didn't, well only peeing on sticks would confirm that outcome.

Things I'd learnt in November

So, what did I learn about my body in November? That she was an evil bitch that's what. After giving me so many symptoms that I was pregnant and then boom: "F**k you Kelly; have your period 7 days late. And just to confuse you even more, we won't give you your normal period just some pink smudge." Seriously? The hubby turned and said, "Don't worry it could be implantation bleeding." Where the hell did that come from? "Google," was his reply. He then turned to me and said "Everything that you've said you've been feeling, I've been Googling to see if it's a sign." What a sweetie he is! Man, I'm so lucky to have this guy in my life and by my side.

So, there it was, for half a day my body got my hopes up again by thinking it could be implantation bleeding, until it came full force. I also learnt that you can get false positives on pregnancy tests called evaporation lines; I had no idea this even existed. I thought a positive was a positive! That happened to me on the Friday; I got my hopes all up and then they were smashed on the Saturday when I got my period. My body doesn't usually cramp either until Mr Blobby is here but nope not that month. I'd been cramping on and off since 4 DPO.

It just goes to show that PMS symptoms are more or less the same as early pregnancy symptoms - according to Google anyway. I think Google had somewhat been my best friend through that month as it had an answer for every symptom known to man. I'm pretty sure that if you had a slight cold you could search and you'd find something that convinced you that you'd got pneumonia. It's amazing how our brains perceive things; even more so when we really want something.

December was fast approaching and so was our upcoming trip to New York! I secretly felt kind of glad that I wasn't pregnant that time. Don't get me wrong, I would have been over the moon if I was but I would've been so worried about flying, even though I know air hostesses fly when they're pregnant so it wouldn't matter too much. To me it wouldn't be worth the risk.

A fiasco in New York City

It had always been on my bucket list to go to The Big Apple at Christmas time and, on our anniversary, the hubby had surprised me with tickets to a Christmas show at Radio City in New York. Dream come true - you'd think. Hmmmmm, maybe not after the vacation we ended up having. What with the airline trying to kill my hubby and ending up in a hotel that was part bloody knocking shop, what else could go wrong? I almost forgot: the hubby got man flu! How I managed to forget that I'll never know as he managed to remind me at least once an hour.

Are you trying to kill my husband?

We fly with the same airline all the time to the USA and we've always found them very accommodating. But not this time. Certainly not this time. We had a short flight to London Heathrow and we were supposed to only have a 5-hour layover. This, however, turned into nearly 12!

A broken-down plane was the first part, with no air-conditioning for 2 hours so even my sweat was sweating at this point. We got told to get off that plane and wait 2 hours for the next one. Ridiculous. At that point, I was starting to get hangry. Being hormonal and stressed out was not a good combination and then add in hunger. After picking up a sandwich from Boots, we decided to sit and wait patiently for 2 hours until our plane finally became available. We found ourselves in another queue to get back on the original plane which had just been put back into use.

Only we weren't going to get on that plane, and all because of free chocolate. My hubby has a severe allergy to peanuts and the airline was made well aware of this; he should've flashed red on their system. Only that didn't happen because there was a fault. And yep, you guessed it, the chocolate that they were handing out contained peanuts. I couldn't believe my eyes. Literally, what were they thinking? Were they trying to kill my hubby off? I always thought that would be my job!

All jokes aside, there was no way that we could get on that plane, knowing that potentially my hubby could lose his life if even one person started to eat peanuts. All we asked for was a call out for passengers to be made aware of his allergy. This was taken into consideration but not obviously dealt with appropriately. That was proved when they started handing out boxes of Celebrations with Snickers in them. Somewhere, someone f***** up big time. The manager that was on at the time was very understanding and helped a lot but we still couldn't get on that flight so we had to wait another 2 hours. But at least then my hubby would be safe. We did in the end get a free upgrade as the flight was somewhat empty. Bonus.

When we arrived in NYC at 1am local time, nearly 11 hours after we were supposed to arrive, we didn't think things could get much worse. Only, they did.

Upon arriving at our hotel, I noticed how grand the lobby looked and thought "this isn't as bad as what TripAdvisor was stating". After 20 minutes of yet more queuing, we headed to the lifts, which looked like something from the 1920s and certainly smelled like it. We got out of the lift onto our floor and approached our room, noticing how bad everything looked and smelt; it had the smell of wet dog. The door to the room looked like an old bank vault door and, at that point, I had very little expectations for the room but, quite frankly, I was so tired that I really didn't care. That was until we walked into it. It was like walking into the 1970's. Only an especially disgusting, dirty and smelly version. There were stains on the walls, stains on the bedding, stains on the curtains, stains in the bathroom, just stains everywhere. I turned to the hubby and said "We're sleeping here for one night then we are looking for a new hotel".

So that's what we did. The next day, we checked out and hopped in a cab and straight into our new digs, which worked out quite well as they were right next to Central Park. The manager there was fabulous and felt so sorry for us after we'd stayed in that shit hole for a night. He even told us some horror stories about the hotel, saying how it was renowned for being the prostitute's choice of hotel. At that point, I realised we'd had a very lucky escape.

After sorting out the hotel fiasco, we decided to do what we came here to do; we became tourists. We visited everything New York had to offer us on a freezing cold tour bus. We had a horse ride in Central Park, a boat ride out to the Statue of Liberty, rode the subway up and down, visited the 9/11 memorial, watched a show on Broadway and, not to mention, all the restaurants and of course the shops! I also finally got to see what I've always wanted to see, the Christmas tree outside of the Rockefeller Centre. Although New York wasn't what I remembered from last time I was here, it was still an amazing place to be. But it was cold - very cold!

I'm glad I can finally say that I've been to New York at Christmas time but I very much doubt that I'd go back. It was far too busy, expensive and commercialised for my liking. Although I still managed to fetch home a NYC fridge magnet, more baubles and a NYPD baby gro for our future Baby Bone. I just couldn't help myself could I? Especially when round 2 would be starting soon. If it hadn't already.

To be or not to be?

"Christmas time, mistletoe and fruit juice". Yes, good old fruit juice because, as much as I wanted to, I wasn't drinking that year because I was on call at work. I know you were all hoping that we'd had our big fat positive but not yet we didn't.

Round 2 was now done and we were awaiting the results. It was so hard not to symptom-spot and pee on as many sticks as I possibly could. 3 down so far and they all said a big fat No! I even dissected one of them, hoping that might actually make a difference but of course it didn't.

Christmas day is different for everyone. To me, it's seeing my family in the morning and exchanging gifts, eating as much crap as you can, and drinking Marks and Spencer bucks fizz. But it was a funny old day because it's not really anything other than any other day. I think my feelings may change when we have our kids opening presents from Santa on Christmas day when the excitement will be there.

Although the excitement for this particular year's Xmas day came when our friends came over for tea with their kids and seeing their excited little faces opening their presents. Now to me, that's what Christmas looks like: wrapping paper strewn everywhere and boxes ripped open and Jacky Boy's Dinos everywhere! I was so excited, I forgot to take any photos!

Christmas day was done and we headed into Boxing Day with no sign of the Wicked Witch. I was officially 2 days late. I had however found out that I have a short luteal phase; which meant I ovulated too late in my cycle for the bean to have a chance to stick, which was just great - another spanner in the works for us.

I was hoping that in the New Year the docs would be able to help us. I didn't have very high hopes for that because all my doctor's did was tell me to lose weight. Like that's the answer to all their problems. Well it was certainly not the answer to mine. I had been told to take vitamin B6 as it was supposed to help so I decided I may try that on my next cycle.

A few days went by; we were now onto the 29th and I had decided that evaporation lines are a twat! Pregnancy test companies need to get it sorted; it was so deceiving. It must pain every woman who is hoping that this month might be her month but then it's swiftly taken away by either: the Wicked Witch rearing her ugly head full flow or retesting, with the hope of seeing another line, and all you get is white - the white that says *not this month*.

I'd made the hubby have sex that night in the hope that it would poke my period out of me, which weirdly usually happens, especially when it is due. I know it was weird but I know a few people who it happened to as well. He turned to me after and said "I don't think it will start". I asked him why and he replied with "Well I only put the tip in!" Well that was it. I was pissing myself laughing.

He said that if there was a baby in there, he didn't want it getting poked by his meat stick. I was crying from laughter. But low and behold, as the morning arrived, so did the evil Wicked Witch and so tampons it was for me that month.

Onto Round 3 with high hopes because 3 is mine and the hubby's lucky number. We had everything crossed that, that time it would work and would stick. Our poor donor would be getting cramp this month. I hope he knew what he'd let himself in for.

Always read the labels

The next month, we decided to up our game and buy a device that is supposed to help aid with conception and, for £70, I thought we may as well try it since it was still cheaper than going to see the doctor!

The Stork at Home Conception Kit is designed to guide a cup, with the sperm inside, to the cervix and can be worn for up to 6 hours. Fabulous I hear you say? That's what we thought too. Well that was until we thought we best practice with it first as, knowing my clumsy self, I would've ended up with the contents everywhere - or worse it stuck up my floof. Could you imagine having to walk around for 6 hours with that stuck up your hoo ha? Yeah, me neither. Practice makes perfect or, so I'd always been told.

Practice makes perfect

Upon opening the contraption, I realised I very much recognised it to have the shape of something that should've been in the Ann Summers' adult only corner and not as a possible baby-making device. So, after chuckling about it being rude looking, I thought that I best crack on and practice on how to use it. The instructions were pretty simple: pull this, push this, push this other doohickey and then it should just sit and stay where it needs to be. So, there it was, tucked up neatly next to my cervix and all the time I was thinking that the next time we do this it would have potential babies inside it.

Always read the labels

It was comfortable when in place and so easy to remove that I thought "I can definitely keep this in place for a good 6 hours; it beats having your legs wrapped around your head for 30 mins." With a quick rinse, it was ready to use again. "So how on earth do you reset it?" The hubby said, "Errrrrm I don't know. Try just shoving it back in the stick or read the instructions." The trouble was, upon reading the instructions, I quickly realised there were no instructions to reset; they only had them to use. I was thinking "well that's stupid; why would you not have instructions to reset?!" Picking up the box to see if there were any more instructions inside, my eyes swiftly scoured the box and noticed that right there, right in the middle of the box, were the words SINGLE USE ONLY. Great not what I needed. Google to the rescue? Nope, for once Google was no help. No one had been as stupid as me and not read the goddamn box. The hubby was like, "It'll be fine I'll find a way." SNAP! Dare I ask what that was? "Errrrrm, I don't think I can find a way. It's broken 100% now."

Who on earth in their right mind would pay £70 for something that could only be used once? If I'd known that, I wouldn't have bothered with the bloody thing. I suppose we learn from our mistakes. Mine being: always read the labels! The worst thing about it all? We found out that the Mooncup is the same thing. You're only paying £70 to not get your fingers messy and you can practice as many times with the Mooncup as it's reusable. We would definitely be trying that on Round 3.

One step forward, three steps back

I sometimes absolutely loathed being a woman. I don't think men realise how easy they've got it. And, for any man about to start reading this chapter, this one is all about periods, hormones, vaginas being probed and clots, lots of clots and so I'm giving you the chance to stop reading now.

Our baby making was currently on hold, due to the fact I'd had not one, not two, but three periods just in the single month alone. I finally plucked up the courage to go to the doctor's and saw a new female doctor, who for once didn't assume that my issues were down to me being slightly on the chunky side. She actually listened to what I had to say and then said that, because I'd not had periods on time for a few months, or that because they'd been so heavy that I just felt like sitting on the toilet all day and especially with the size of the clots that were coming out of me, she was sending me for tests. These were the kind of tests that every woman dreads having: having the massive probe (ultrasound stick) shoved up your hoo ha. Now, that's not my issue; my issue is that because of the amount of KY Jelly they smother it in first, the squelch noise it makes as it probes your fanny, sends a shiver down my spine and not in a good way! Then, for the rest of the day, I usually spend most of it running to the toilet to mop up (pass me the bread).

Then I had to go to have a smear test done. Most women avoid having this because they actually have to show the doctor's their lady parts. But I've had that many doctors prodding and poking my vagina now, I'm past caring and well over the embarrassment. What most women don't realise is, this test is done to potentially save your life and doctors don't care if you've not trimmed the lady garden for a few months, or years, or if you like it a little extra fluffy because they see these types of things day in, day out. All I would suggest is maybe a quick scrub, a dub, dub with a bit of Femfresh. You wouldn't like the doctor smelling a fish supper, would you?

The doctor was also sending me for blood tests because, with me having Polycystic Ovary Syndrome, my hormone levels could get out of sync, to the point where I didn't know when my next period would be, or if I was even actually going to have one that month. It would also tell them whether I was ovulating or not, which at that time, I didn't think I was because the OPK's aka pee sticks were saying not.I was also having pains in my ovaries, which I thought was ovulation but it turned out that it may have been a cyst bursting so the blood test and the ultrasound would confirm this either way.

I was hoping that it wouldn't be a long drawn out process as we all know how quick the NHS is to send out appointment letters. Once it was all done and I'd had the all clear, we planned to be back onto the baby making process. I just felt like I was taking one step forward and three steps back.

Just Breathe

This chapter isn't like my normal ones; it's not a jokey one. As far as this is a laughing matter, if I don't write how I was feeling, I felt like I was going down that spiral and I didn't want to hit the bottom; I'm talking about depression.

I would love to call this 'thing' an illness. But just when you think you're getting better, it's back with a vengeance, back to hit you harder than you've ever felt. That feeling where you feel like you're drowning in your own emotion, tears and sorrow. The questions that float around your swirling mind: *when will this ever end? When will I feel better again? Why is this happening to me? Is it normal to feel like this?* You answer yourself and every question, with a whirlwind of helpless answers, desperately trying to make sense of it all, desperately trying to make yourself feel a little better, but in turn, you question your own answers, your own thoughts, and your own mind.

This was how I was feeling at the time when I was writing this: like I was drowning but just about keeping my head above water, smiling day in, day out, through the tears that pricked my eyes. My bed was where I went for peace and quiet, dreading the fact I would have to get up and actually face the world for another day. Did anyone judge me for this? No. Did anybody see my pain? No. And, why, I hear you ask? Because I had become a master at hiding it. I didn't want pity. I don't want you to feel sorry for me. I just want you to realise that you're not alone in feeling the way you do. I know a lot of people in my position are feeling the way I was, desperately seeking answers for the way they feel, knowing that if you go to the doctor's you think that you're admitting failure. But, the thing is, you're not admitting it to the doctor, you're admitting it to yourself.

Well that appointment was made for me. I had been off my 'happy meds', as I call them, for a couple of months because I'd wanted to be drug free for baby making. And after having counselling and finishing my treatment, I thought I didn't need them anymore as I'd felt somewhat normal. Only, I know now that they were masking everything I felt. I felt numb to the world and my surroundings and I wanted to feel again. Only now I had started feeling, it wasn't the feeling I had hoped for. I knew going back on happy pills wasn't the solution to my problems but they did help me see clearly so I could understand what was going on in my brain. Being off them, my brain felt foggy again and, as much as I searched for the light, I couldn't quite reach it yet. So I was hoping that on a low dosage, I might not have been as numb as what I was the first time I was on them, and that I might then even be able to sort my own head out and get rid of the fog and see the light at the end of the tunnel. So I would feel like yet again I could just breathe.

Period drama

I decided that upon my next heavy monthly cycle, I would test the Mooncup out in place of tampons and fanny pads (aka sanitary towels), in preparation for when we would use it on round 3. Obviously, I was going to have two separate Mooncups: one for spunk collecting and one for the good old menstrual flow.

Now because I had PCOS, I had an incredibly heavy monthly cycle. The kind where you think you're dying because the pain is THAT bad and the amount of blood that actually comes out could paint someone's wall!

Regarding the pain, I always found that pushing a tampon up there hurts like hell because I'm sure that it pokes my cervix and I just can't seem to get it in the right place. Obviously, I know it's in the right hole, but you know it's not right when you have to do that funny walk, a bit like John Wayne, hoping that it will readjust on its own account. Only it doesn't, and you have to push and pull a bit more and then get flustered because it's still just not right, before finally yanking it out shouting "f**k you" and replacing it with a fanny pad.

Then the fanny pad drama begins. With wings or without wings? Can I wear the night-time ones for daytime? Not that your period cares whether it's night or day anyway. Mine likes to attack me in the middle of the night when I least expect her to arrive. And then boom there she flows. I much prefer the winged type as the wingless ones seem to get all creased up and I'm constantly having to readjust, even in public, due to the fact that either my butt crack is swallowing it or my foof is. After several readjustments, that also gets ripped off, with a firm "f**k you" as it slam dunks into the bin. Tampon to the rescue. Then the drama starts all over again.

Don't even get me started on the drama of the rattling packets in a public toilet. It's almost as bad as putting as much loo roll down the toilet so you can have a poop in public and be relieved not to hear that embarrassing splash. I know most of you do it, whether you like to admit it or not. Not that anyone gives a damn. What else is a toilet for? Everyone poops and most people have the rattling fanny pad packet that they are trying to open, so slowly, trying not to sound like you're ripping strips of duct tape because heaven forbid that the little old lady in the next cubicle, farting away to herself, hears it and now knows that you're on your period. What do you think is going to happen? That the old lady is going to shout out, "Oh I hear you're on your period dear. What brand do you use? Back in my day, we had to buy ours from behind the counter, you know; it's not like these days when you can buy them from any old shop and even the toilets sell them for 50p I'll have you know." Of course that's not going to happen because no one cares. But man, I still hate public toilets and rustling fanny packets.

So, here it was, the answer to all my prayers, my saviour: the Mooncup. A funny little thing it was. Its packaging greatly offended me when trying to pick a size, as it read: "size A for over 30's or vaginal birth and size B for under 30's or C-section". Well, I'm over 30 and don't have any kids so does that mean that because I'm over 30, I have a bigger fandango than a woman who's under 30? The more I thought about it, the more I started to worry that the older I get, the bigger my flower will get. (Cue shit loads of pelvic floor exercises, as I'm not ready to have, or to even think about having a bat cave for a vajayjay!)

After standing in Boots debating about the size of my vagina, I decided that even though I was 31, I had the vagina of a younger woman and so size B was handed over to the lady at the counter. And, as if by magic, my body must have heard me talking period drama and *boom* there she was: my 4th period in 2 months. I then needed to test the fitting of my Mooncup and, as if by magic, it fitted. I'm pleased to announce that whilst the rest of my body might have been getting older and wider, my little tuppence was staying just that - little.

To get to the point, I would definitely recommend the Mooncup. I think the only downside to it is that I now get to measure how much blood I'm actually losing. And, I really don't think that the amount that I'm actually losing is normal or at least Google says it's not. I decided that I must also discuss that with the doctor when I saw them next week.

Getting back to the point once again, as I'm a devil for deviating, the Mooncup is so comfortable to wear. And, as big as it looks, you really can't feel it in there. Mine was a bloody good fit if I haven't mentioned it already. I fit in the small size - rather proud of that if you hadn't guessed. It does half suction itself to your cervix though, which in turn I suppose is a good thing because you don't want any spillages. I haven't luckily had any yet, even wearing it at night-time.

So, here's to no more tampon drama, or rattling fanny pads that feel like they are going to disappear up your butt crack and here's to the little (there's that word again) Mooncup: my period drama is no more.

Drama at the doctor's surgery

There I was, sat on my sofa, catching up on the latest episode of Master Chef, with 2 pints of water and a cup of tea sloshing around in my bladder, waiting patiently for the clock to hit 14:30. God forbid the doctor's were running late as I didn't know how much longer I could go without peeing. It's even worse when you know you're not allowed to pee. But worse than that still, I needed a poo and you can't poop without peeing. And I couldn't not poop in case I then had the urge to fart when the poor ultrasound technicians would be in direct line.

Dilemma at its finest so what did I do? I rang me mam and told her my predicament. The outcome was to have a poo and drink shit loads more water in hope that they could still do the ultrasound because I don't think I could've lived down the shame of farting in the doctor's office.

I thought that the next time I would have an ultrasound, I would be looking at my little alien. In every scan photo I've ever seen, the baby always looks like those squishy little jelly aliens you used to play with as a 90's kid. The ones you were told that if you stick their arses together and stick them in the fridge they would get pregnant. There was always that one kid that had the babies. Liar.

Well I wasn't looking at my jelly alien baby, or even an actual baby, I was looking at my ovarian cysts because I thought that one of them decided to rupture last month. Usually, according to the doctor's, it can cause some slight discomfort and a bit of bleeding, not to the point where I'm doubled over trying not to be sick from the pain, but uncomfortable. Mine was almost as bad as period pain but one-sided and I'd had 4 periods in 4 weeks. I was sure that wasn't normal!

So I sat in the doctor's office, trying not to think about water, toilets or water in toilets so as not to pee myself. I was clock watching: 14:31, 14:32, 1433...14:33...14:33. Then I heard the magic words: my name. If I could've jumped in the air, I would've; except if I had tried, I would have either peed or exploded!

Walking into the ultrasound office, I was met by two smiling faces and I automatically relaxed. Thankfully, it was over in 30 minutes and part of the results were in. I was curious as to how big my little cysts were growing; 1.9cm was the biggest, which I know sounds quite big but considering they don't act until they are 3cm I'd say I was pretty safe at that moment even if I was in pain.

My next examination was the smear test, which I know a lot of women don't like getting done but it's so important and it's not like a doctor's not seen a vagina before. The first smear I had to cancel and rearrange due to me bleeding yet again; the second one was cancelled due to the doctor not having their code for the test and then that particular day was take 3.

After getting up at 8am, freshening up my daisy and making sure my lady garden was prepared to perfection, I was ready. Arriving at the surgery, I was called through to be asked "Why are you here today? How can I help you?" Confused as I was with the question, I replied with "Well I was supposed to be here for a smear test, but obviously you're not aware of this?" Yet again I was told that the doctor didn't have her code either and neither did the other female doctor that was in the surgery. Now I'm no doctor, but I work in a safety-critical environment and if my competencies aren't up to date, then I can't work. So, why - why can a doctor's surgery not be organised enough to have their doctors up to date with a simple code so that they can perform an important test? It is beyond me!

So, there I was, having to juggle my shifts and try to book another test in. To some this may sound simple but I mainly work 07:00-19:00 and 19:00-07:00 and my doctor's surgery opens at 8 and closes at 6! They also then had to find me a doctor who is equipped with their code. I simply said to the doctor that I was not bothered whether it was a male or female doctor; I just wanted it done.

My particular annoyance was that there are so many women who fear getting this done and, if one of them had been in my shoes, I'm pretty sure that they would've just not turned up. And, to be honest with the farce of it all, I was pretty damn annoyed that I'd wasted 2 appointments that could've been avoided. A bit of organisation goes a long way.

So I had to wait until the next week when I would hopefully have all of my results to decide if I needed to see the specialist again and if anything else needed to be done. Otherwise Round 3 would soon be around the corner.

Sssh I've got a secret

I have had a secret since last March and until now I'd not wanted to share it due to being embarrassed as it has such a stigma against it.

After being told time, and time, and time again that I needed to lose weight and, no matter how hard I tried, losing 7 or 8 pounds, the weight just would not move. I had doctor's telling me that it would affect my fertility. I had them telling me it would affect my health. I had them telling me I was hitting the 'morbidly obese' category. Who wants to hear that? All I heard was "You're a lazy fat f**k". But, let me tell you, I'm far from lazy. I'm non-stop from morning until evening. Some days I feel like I've got ants in my pants, only sitting down to have a quick brew.

I'd tried Weight Watchers, Slimming World, the Cambridge Diet, Atkins Diet, going to my favourite swear word "the gym", walking, not eating after a certain time, I even tried the awful tablets that the doctor's give out, that make you shit yourself if you eat anything of slight fat content - God, they were the devil - but even following the plan I couldn't even nip it. Even more embarrassing, when you're at work and have to ring the old lady across the way to ask if I could borrow a spare pair of underwear. It was a good job she was so understanding. I tried these diets with the same determination throughout every single one of them. Only, I could lose 7 pounds or so and then I would get stuck no matter what I did. I even stopped eating for a few days and gained weight! Nothing worked, nothing helped, and I was starting to lose my motivation and also my mind.

I'd read every post about diet and exercise and my condition because having PCOS and trying to lose weight is like battling a war that cannot be won. It's almost impossible unless you're so strict that you may as well not even bother eating.

The research continues

So after our first appointment with the fertility clinic last January, and being told yet again that I was too fat, I decided enough was enough. We wanted a baby so badly that I would do anything and I took the matter into my own hands.

I started researching weight loss surgeries and only my hubby knew what I was pondering because I didn't feel comfortable telling family and friends. There's always been such a stigma with myself and weight loss surgeries as I thought someone that would do that was weak and lazy. But, in fact, it's the complete opposite. It's sheer desperation. It's sheer determination. It's all mixed in with that little sprinkle of hope. It's a last resort. It was my last resort.

I knew that I had some savings put away which were supposed to be for our IUI procedure so I was in a dilemma. I was in a dilemma because I couldn't have the IUI without losing the weight and I couldn't afford both.

It was tough but I made up my mind and booked the appointment. I was aware that I had to be a certain weight, well BMI, for them to consider me for surgery and, with this information, I found out I was actually underweight for something. I don't think I'd ever been so shocked. So, what do you do in a situation like that? There were two options: either give up and feel sorry for myself, or gain weight. It was only 6 pounds. How hard could it be? I had two weeks to do it.

However, for once, I found it hard to gain the weight, no matter what I ate! Heavy clothes adorned and a belly full of food, I attended the appointment with hubby in toe. I came out of that doctor's surgery full of hope and optimism, knowing that in just a few months I could be skinny again but would I be happy?

I'd never really been super skinny. I've always battled with my weight and my demons surrounding it. It had been made even worse in the past as I had people in my life that were unsympathetic and unsupportive and made me feel fat even despite only being around a UK 10. I was told I was fat and worthless and I started to believe it. I was pressured into going to the gym and losing weight, to the point I was making myself sick after every meal but, when they found that out, I was told it was the cheat's way out and had to stop. Nothing I did was ever good enough for that person and no amount of weight I lost was praised, or even accounted for. So, after suffering for almost 7 years of emotional abuse, I left. Unfortunately, the scars have stayed with me. Even with the hubby being as supportive as he is, I couldn't help but feel I was letting him down as my weight was stopping us from the chance of being parents.

The decision was made and the operation was booked. I knew it wasn't going to be easy, and the road ahead was long, but the results were something that I was quite looking forward to. I wanted to try and see the results from the surgery and so I decided to document my progress in picture form every week, from the night before surgery until now. I was so hopeful that the surgery was my answer, but even after putting my body through that, and losing nearly 3 stone, my BMI was still too high and I was left hardly being able to eat anything or, if I did eat, being sick from eating too quickly, or drinking whilst eating, or not chewing my food properly. The food I once loved, I now hated. And for what? To please the doctor's? To be able to look at myself and not feel like a failure?

The only good thing about getting the surgery is that I now couldn't overindulge or comfort eat because the band would stop me. The downside was I couldn't go for a nice meal without having to take a sick bag; it used to be a doggy bag. Although, for once in my life, I actually struggled to put weight on, and hallelujah to that!

So that's my secret now exposed about how my weight loss happened at such a quick rate and how I'd kept it off. People can think what they like about it. All I know is, I wouldn't look back. And I would do it all over again to be able to have the chance, albeit a slim one, to have a baby. I still had about a stone to lose before Manchester would take us on and that's if our turkey baster method failed. Here was me hoping that Round 3 worked because, after all, it seemed to be my lucky number.

Shit happens, then you get over it

For an entire month I felt like we'd been treading on eggshells because of an impending diagnosis and, for once, it wasn't for me; it was for the hubby.

In that February, we were told in the doctor's office that there was a possibility that the hubby could have throat cancer. Right there and then, when the words came out of the doctor's mouth, I felt my stomach creep into mine. With a million and one questions going through my mind, the words just couldn't exit my mouth. I was choked. The hubby sat there, at first in silence, and then started asking questions but, as the doctor had no idea what it was, he had to go for the worst case scenario and couldn't answer the majority of them. He was put on the emergency theatre list and that was that.

After leaving the hospital, I just didn't know what to say to him so I decided not to mention it and the car journey home was very much in silence. I thought I would keep my thoughts to myself unless he brought it up. It was my coping mechanism; it had been for years, to bottle everything up deep down inside and lock it away, with a key that only I can unlock when, and only if, I felt like it.

A few days passed in a blur and the weekend was in full flow and yet all I could think about was *what if? What if it was cancer? What if they found it too late? What if he gets told he only has months to live?* Then again, on the other hand, I was thinking: *what if it was nothing? What if it's just a simple infection? Loads of people get that, don't they? Is our insurance up to date and shit? We don't have a will in place. Would I be able to afford the mortgage on my own and cover the bills?*

This year was supposed to be our fresh start, with babies on the way and now it felt like I was in a f*****g soap opera drama on TV but we didn't have the scripts to find out the outcome. I think I knew deep down that the hubby was thinking the exact same things as I was so I pulled myself together and asked him the simple question: what if?

After spending most of our Saturday afternoon discussing finances and our will that we need to put in place, I realised that, even though I was renowned for being 'Little Miss Organised', when it came to the prospect of one, or both, of us dying we weren't prepared at all. I mean, at the age of 31, who was thinking about death? I think at that point we were both relieved to talk about it as the pressure was starting to get to us both in different ways. At that point we hadn't even told family or friends because frankly there was nothing to tell, not until we knew something more than what we already knew.

Valentine's Day came and went; we don't celebrate it; it's a load of commercialised shit if you ask me. If you can't show your other half that you love them everyday then there's something wrong there like!

February 15th was the day the reality really hit; it was the day the hubby's operation date came through - and it was in less than a month. I shouldn't really call it an 'operation' as it was a biopsy but, because of where it is, he would have to be under general anaesthesia - so to me that was an operation. I wasn't sure what to expect after he had his 'operation' so I decided to do some research on, cue, you guessed it: Dr Google. I don't know why I bothered as after reading all the information I realised that even Google had no idea either and that's saying something.

February came and went in a blur. With 2 weeks until the hubby's impending op, the strain was starting to get to me. However, I couldn't show it because I had to be strong for him. He had read that he may not have been able to talk for up to two weeks after his surgery which we laughed off at the time and I joked it would be nice to have a bit of peace and quiet but, in the back of my mind, I was thinking this shit is getting real. It got especially so when I started the weekly shop online and realised that he may not be able to eat solid food. I was scrolling through the items online to figure out what's soft but not baby food: soup and ice-cream it was then!

The week of his op was supposed to be a celebration for us as we would have been dating for 6 years. We would usually celebrate it by going for a nice meal on the night. Not this year though as, with all that in the air, I'd forgotten about it.

The night before his op, we went out to take both our minds off of the situation. The night passed quickly and it was suddenly time to get up and go. Dropping the hubby off at the hospital felt like torture; I felt awful for having to leave him all on his own but, as it was classed as day surgery, it meant no visitors; so cue a few falling tears as I drove away.

Pulling home onto the drive and not knowing what will happen within the next few hours is something that I really don't want to go through again. And, if it wasn't for the bestie, Sarah, taking my mind off it all day, I think I would've been climbing the walls; especially when it got to 6pm and I'd not heard anything yet. All I knew was that he went down for his op at 4pm and they said it would take roughly an hour. I couldn't wait any longer so I rang the hospital; at least if they could tell me he was out of surgery I would be a little bit relieved. But I got the opposite. The nurse had no idea who, or where the hubby was and I got told to phone back in 30 minutes. So that I did: 30 minutes later and I received the same response; they had no idea where the hubby was; if he'd even come out of surgery, or anything at all. All they could tell me was that he would be coming down to their ward eventually and I needed to phone back at 7pm.

In a panicked state, I realised that I was meant to be at work the next day at 7am. I knew I was in no fit state for that so I had to ring the oncall to get cover, which luckily there was. After all the phone calls, it was at that point, when I was getting my shoes on and I was ready to go down and play holy hell with them, that I got the text - the text that made me sigh with relief - and all it was, was a picture of toast captioned "Mmmmm toast". He was okay and eating.

After getting sent the picture of toast and starting to feel somewhat relieved, I then got another text that read: "You can be the bearer of good news, I don't have Mr C. They didn't find anything unto ord, so other than feeling like I have had my head ripped off and kicked round a field and stuck back on I'm all tickety boo xxxx".

No words came from my mouth; I just cried, and cried. The tears that I'd held back for over a month were coming out and they weren't stopping. The sick feeling that had been looming, gone.

All I wanted to do then was hug the hubby but they were debating whether they would let him out that night. His oxygen level wouldn't go above 70% and, as he's asthmatic, that wasn't good at all. I was told that I would have to wait until 10pm to find out if he was able to come home. 10pm came and went and then finally I got the text: "I'm ready for pick up. Come and get me." Well, at least at that time there's no traffic so I had a clear run through to York.

Upon picking him up, I didn't dare hug him because he looked so frail. And I knew that if I had hugged him, I wouldn't be able to control my emotions and nobody wanted to see Kelly's crying face in the hospital. So I waited until we got home and then held him so tight; I was frightened to let go.

It's amazing how I felt that we had been taking life for granted each and every day. Our story could've been worse - a lot worse - but here we are stronger than ever. When shit happens, you really do just have to get over it and move on or it will consume you.

Happy smiley faces

Well after those last few months, things couldn't get any bloody worse; could they really? January, February and March were officially written off. So I was thinking, "Hello April, you gorgeous looking month. I hope you have some good news in store for me." We would see.

At the end of March, after I'd decided that the beginning of the year could officially kiss my arse, we decided to take a trip to re-energise and recharge our batteries. Only, that's not quite what happened. The place we picked was London, of all places, the busy capital city, and, of all the times to go, we went when Brexit was happening. We somehow even managed to accidentally walk in the protest march. Now, I'm not going to get started on the whole political palaver, as to me that's frankly quite boring but let's just say it was especially busy that weekend and the crowds were manic.

So, what did we do, apart from walk millions of miles, as Kelly didn't quite check the location of the hotel like she thought she had? I thought it was close to the tube and Big Ben because that's what it looked like on the map. It was like a fingernail size away so presumably I thought it was rather close by.

Getting off the tube at Pimlico, (quite liked saying that) and realising that there were no taxis and, we had a good 10-15min walk in shoes that I really shouldn't have worn. They are that type of shoe that are too cute not to buy but hurt like a bitch to wear. All I could do was moan, and you can ask my hubby about that - if he's even removed his earplugs yet. We eventually arrived at the hotel in a nice quiet area. This was just what we needed as we literally had no plans for the weekend.

Although I really, really wanted to go to Harrods to see the puppies and to eat cake; because who doesn't love puppies and cake? Never mind the clothes and shoes, cake and puppies are the way forward. So off to Harrods we went. We searched on every floor and could only find cake; they didn't have the puppies anymore. I felt so sad. Luckily the cake sure cheered me up. I also had to drag the hubby around the baby section, just to show him which pushchair I would like - if we won the lottery - it was gold and it was beautiful. It even had the matching highchair - also in gold!

After realising that we had spent pretty much our entire afternoon in Harrods, my feet were aching so much. Although this was partly because my dumb ass had forgotten to put socks on. Luckily there was a shop close by to help me out and then Starbucks to give me that much needed caffeine boost.

We could then go on to enjoy our evening in the casino. An hour on the tube and £50 later, I'd decided we needed cocktails. Only, I didn't realise that I would end up wearing the bloody thing. I wasn't even drunk. Just clumsy. After downing half of it, I got up out of my swivel chair, tried to take a sip and then, smack: the chair had swung round and hit me, sending my drink flying half down my throat and the rest all over my face. Yes, I had just swilled myself. A round of applause to me. We decided to call it a night.

The next day, we spent half of it just strolling around, getting - I would say our bearings - but we just got lost and ended up in yet another casino; there's far too many in London. This one however was my all-time favourite as, not only did it have my favourite game in it, Casino Wars, but I actually got asked for my ID. I have never felt so young. It must've been the new haircut. The only time that I felt rich there was when I went to the cash machine to withdraw some money and out popped a £50 note. Who the hell has ever seen one of them before? They're like rocking horse poop, or toilet paper for rich people.

The afternoon came upon us and it was time to meet up with one of the hubby's old friends but I won't say that he's old just in case he's reading. But it was a friend that he'd known for a long time. That day was the day I was going to break my, 'I'm not drinking, because I don't want to scupper the chances of getting pregnant'. That day I was determined to get drunk to that feeling where you feel like you're slightly floating, but yet still grounded; that was the feeling I aimed for. Sure to say, I can't actually remember the rest of that evening due to the consumption of far too many Pornstar Martinis flowing down my neck. Which, in turn means I had a good night.

Round 3

Getting home, I realised it was that time of the month for when I needed to pee on sticks, sticks and more sticks. Getting slightly frustrated at the fact my ovulation was far too late in my cycle, we came home on what would be my cycle (day 19), and most normal people ovulate on cycle day 14/15, but nope, not me, I was nowhere near. The line was so faint I had to squint just to make it out.

I thought, "Here we go again. Give me a break, please. I'm not going to ovulate again." Oh, how wrong I was. On cycle day 22 I got my happy smiley face on the clear blue ovulation tests. I'd only ever had this once before, back in November, so hopes were high. I also got it for 3 days running this time which was fabulous. It basically meant that I had 24 to 72 hours before the egg was officially released. And, because I have a 35/37 day cycle, it was about the right time for me.

All we had to do was give our donor a shout. Of course, he came through for us yet again. (There's a pun in there somewhere I'm sure). This time round we were more prepared than the last two, as I think we all knew what we were doing. I also changed our method slightly, so I had more of a chance of keeping the little swimmers up there longer, by using the Mooncup. Of course this was a different one to that one which I use for the time of the month. My thoughts were, "If it was good enough to keep blood escaping, it was good enough to keep the swimmers up there longer." It was also literally pushed up against my cervix opening so they didn't have far to go.

So Round 3 was officially over and we were now awaiting the results. A long 14 days we would have to wait until I could pee on yet more sticks. We were hoping it would be good news so it would be the best birthday present I've ever gotten. Or if it wasn't, then at least I could have a very merry birthday!

I should've been called Annie

I'm so impatient when it comes to waiting for anything, even more so when I was waiting to pee on sticks or for Mr Blobby to rear its ugly head. My Mam and Dad should've called me Annie and I would've definitely lived up to the phrase of being an impatient one!

We had officially entered the two week wait for Round 3 and I needed to keep myself busy so I didn't start peeing on sticks far too early again. At least I knew that I definitely ovulated on cycle day 25 which, despite being quite late for some people, for me it was about right. Having a 35 to 37 day cycle would give it plenty of time to become a sticky bean.

1-3 DPO: I felt literally nothing. I felt almost normal. Then 4 DPO I started to spot. I was thinking, "For f***s sake; we're out again. This is just getting old now!" So, there I was, running to the toilet to do knicker checks every two mins to see if it had changed colour, or Mr Blobby had full on shown up early, but nope nothing.

5 DPO and the spotting from day 4 had stopped and was now a lovely white squelch. I started to relax again and I started to think our luck was perhaps changing, that this might have actually been our month. Oh what a thought. It would've been a Christmas Day due date.

Back to reality, and all I felt was slight cramping. There were almost spasm-like pains in my back and right side. I did eventually put that down to overdoing it at the gym. Oh yeah, I almost forgot to say, I had gotten used to my favourite swear word twice a week - sometimes 3 if I was really lucky!

The bestie had been nagging me to go with her for months, and I was like, "No way! Not a chance you will see me in that place." But I caved and we found a quiet gym, literally. It was like a ghost town, partially because nearly all the machines are broken; it could probably do with condemning. I was actually waiting for the day that I would end up falling through the ceiling but we made the most of it. I really think me and Sarah just went there for a good rant, and a rave with our cheesy pop songs and Clubland. I mean to workout to.

One of the days, we were ranting, and putting the world to rights, and I was openly talking about sex and insemination, you know all the things friends talk about, and then I heard it; the metal clanging together from the weights room. Shit we weren't alone. Boy did we chuckle. They must've thought we were a right pair of randy buggars! Not like I was particularly bothered, I really needed that rant.

6 DPO and here came the list of symptoms from my symptom spotter. None. I felt absolutely nothing at all. This was rather odd for me as, usually a week before The Witch arrives, I'm plagued with serious PMT. Could it have been a sign? I was resisting peeing on sticks until the weekend was over and I would be at least 10 DPO as I only had one First Response test left and just couldn't

think about paying another £10 for something I was literally going to throw in the bin.

I had about 20 cheapies that came with my other pee sticks, so I considered cracking that packet open. I knew that once I started peeing on them, I would turn into a full blown, raging self-confessed 'pee-on-a-stick addict'. (Yes that is a thing). I would do it until I either got that second little line, or The Witch punched me in the vag!

Okay, okay, okay. So I caved and broke my 'don't pee on sticks rule'. And what happened? A guaranteed negative happened and a shift in my mood. So 7 DPO was negative and I was a moody bitch. Also I had nipples that represent torpedo shoots and they were relentless. I would usually only get this when I was seriously cold and they would always go back to normal after I've warmed up. But not at that minute. The first and only thing I want to do when I enter the house is whip that 'over the shoulder boulder holder off' and ping it in a corner somewhere. Sheer bliss.

8 DPO and I wasn't peeing on sticks. I wasn't peeing on sticks! So, guess what I did? I peed on sticks. I'd entered the official status of POAS (pee on a stick) addict. And guess what the outcome of that was: yep negative again. I didn't like this game anymore. I never won. I also looked about 6 months pregnant with the amount of bloating I had going on. If only it had been real and not a bloat baby.

9 DPO and I woke up with cramps. And I mean cramps; the type you get just before rag week hits. I felt gloomy but I was dragged to Costco as we needed food. I had a lovely hour trip to buy the most random of shit: butter, juice and seaweed - which I can tell you now made me gag. It's foul smelling and tastes like a dead fish! Never eating that again! I decided that, once again, the two week wait can kiss my arse!

Why do they make pregnancy symptoms the same as PMS? Sore boobs, craving anything sugary and cramps. I mean, come on, I'm sure whoever created this whole fertility thing didn't think this one through, did they? If it's pregnancy, you should just puke and have sore boobs and then you'd just know. Whereas if it's PMS, you should have cramps. The mother f***ing cramps and then you'd know that your period is just saying hello.

Also, I peed on a stick just to make sure that the previous day's negative was still a negative and my squinty invisible line eyes weren't deceiving me again. 10 DPO meant 2 more days until Mr Blobby arrived and, so far, there was no sign. Not a drop. So either she was just going to turn up full flow, or maybe, just maybe?

I decided not to pee on a stick that morning. Nah, just kidding I peed in a cup instead and dipped the stick. The results were in: a big fat negative. I'd had the weirdest dream that night: *I dreamt I was going to get my nails done and her little girl was sick and it was also during the bank holidays. I was peeing on sticks and it instantly turned positive.* If only dreams were real.

11 DPO: I was working at night so didn't get to pee on a stick until the morning. I'd decided I wasn't testing until the 20th when I would be 14 DPO and that was if Aunt Flow didn't show. It was driving me up the wall. I didn't feel like my period was imminent but it was supposed to be due the next day. Knowing my luck, it'd be a month my PCOS decided that it would take over and make me a week late.

So, until the 20th hits I would not pee on any more sticks. I'd hidden them and it wouldn't take me long to forget where. When I'm on nights, my brain cells like to fart and f**k off.

I had my fingers crossed for an optimistic outcome but if not, I would get to see the specialist the next month to try and get my ovulation and periods under control. Hopefully they would make me normal with the simple medication again.

Time to gear it up a notch

When life gives you lemons, make sangria. I was feeling sorry for myself because The Witch turned up, punched me in the vag and made me bleed. The bitch. In other news, I was another year older. Another year had gone by and our family was still incomplete. My entire birthday was spent at work, a whole 12 hours worth of my day. I'd almost stopped celebrating my birthday now; what was there to celebrate? That I was getting old?

I'd got home from work to find the post on my doorstep, including a lovely letter from the NHS requesting my presence and another meeting for them to inspect my fandango yet again as they didn't quite get enough cells on my last smear test. So ankles together, knees apart, and deep breath once again... fabulous! It was hopefully 5th time lucky for this one, considering the rigmarole I'd had last time, with my GP not having the required documents to do my smear.

Round 4 was going to be happening within the next few weeks and it would hopefully be 4th time lucky. I'd been doing some research for this round in order to help our chances of implantation. One of the things I'd read up on is taking a low dose aspirin a day as apparently it can help the cervical fluid to become more accommodating for the little swimmers. It's also good for low grade inflammation. Which takes me onto my next bit of research: foods that help whilst trying to conceive. Pineapple has a natural inflammatory enzyme within its core and is most effective when eaten during ovulation and up to 5 DPO. It looked like it was going to be tropical smoothies for the next week or so. Bring it on.

Slow down.

So I went round to my besties to have a rant about: not being pregnant; round 3 failing and some other random shit I just needed to vent about. It wasn't like me to have a moan those days. I was starting to feel like a whiny old woman, especially after being miserable all day on my birthday due to not wanting to become another year older. It felt like only yesterday I'd turned 31, and I was thinking that my life seems to be flying by, and now another year had zoomed past in a blink.

So back to my rant. I'd walked into Laura's house armed with cake, which I snuck into the fridge so that the kids didn't see it because they would've been going to bed soon and I didn't think cake before bed was a particularly good idea. I've found that kids and sugar don't mix well. So whilst the kids did their thing, me and Laura were putting the world to rights, and laughing over the fact that my big butt had nearly gotten me in trouble the other day:

After spending nearly 2 hours clothes shopping in town with Sarah, my feet, back and body ached so I'd decided that, whilst Sarah was in yet another changing room, I would help myself to the chair in the next one. Only it hadn't quite gone to plan. Whilst dragging the chair, my giant ba-donka-donk had hit the wall, making a rather large bang and, the next thing I knew, the curtain and pole had been on top of me! I would've laughed but inside I was dying of shame and scurried into the empty changing room.

So, there I was, sitting and waiting to be asked "What do you think of this?" Now I'm someone who will tell you the honest truth. If I think it's a damn ugly dress, that's what I will say. I don't hold back and I expect the same back. So, whilst I was sitting and waiting for that phrase, this woman had walked into the other changing room and was trying on this God-awful dress. Then the words came out of her mouth, "What do you think of this?" Now, this is someone I'd never met before and I thought to myself, "Do I tell her it's disgusting or do I tell her it's lovely?" Of course, I wasn't going to sit there and say it looked nice so I thought I'd go for the "It's a little on the big side isn't it?" Her reply was, "Well I'm getting it anyway." Well why bloody waste my time and ask me for an opinion if you didn't want it? Stupid woman!

So, remember the cake I was telling you about, Phoebe found it and we had to share cake. Goddamn it! I'm sure kids have cake radars that go "beep, beep, beep" when they sense that there's cake or sweeties nearby. It's like when I go into the dog's treat cupboard; he doesn't hear his own name being called but, by God, can he hear that cupboard door opening; he's in the room like a bloody flash!

After sharing our cakes, it was time for Sir Jacky Boy's bedtime. After countless "night,nights" and slobbery kisses, he was gone. That was, until we were just getting into a rather juicy gossip session, and then in toddled Jack, plonking his butt on the sofa, with a huge smirk on his face. Well, we both looked at each other and went, "What! How did you get out of your cot?" He just smiled that smile which translates to "I'm so proud of myself right now". It was so amusing!

Taking him back to bed, we just had to see how he got out and he was more than willing to show us. He'd managed to pull his body weight up onto the changing table and then just plopped on the floor with a 'ta-da' expression. We stood there mesmerised at how he managed to do it. He was only 2 years old. Too young for a big boy bed surely? Or maybe not.

We decided to move the changing table, as it was getting late, and we thought it would deter him from his Houdini act. But, oh no, not Jack. We'd been downstairs for no longer than 5 minutes before he strolled into the living room once more. He's one determined kid; I'll give him that! Laura realised that they didn't have a baby gate to stop him getting out so a 9pm trip to Aldi it was. Luckily, they had one left in the baby event, and it had Jack's name all over it!

Getting back to their house, we realised that we'd have to take the crib to pieces. And then reassemble it again as the bed. Well if you could've seen what we were up to, you would have pissed yourself laughing. We were trying to unscrew, re-screw, put that in the right hole, put that in the other hole - the whole thing turned into one big innuendo. We had to keep stopping as we just kept laughing at each other.

Eventually, an hour later, he was all tucked up in his big boy bed and all I could think of was, "slow down little man. You're growing up too quickly." I still remember getting the 3am text to say he had been born. Time flies far too quickly so enjoy it; enjoy every second of it!

Help! I have vagina issues.

Opening my letters, I noticed one that looked like it was from the hospital. I'm one of those weird people who can guess where my mail is from, especially around my birthday; I know exactly who's sent me a card and also who's not getting one this year!

Anyway, I ripped open my, oh lucky here, I was right, NHS letter, to end up completely melting down in tears. If you remember me telling you, back in January I had vagina issues. I'd had 4 periods in the space of one month followed by weird bleeding the two months after that. Anyway, I'd been to see my GP and they'd said they were sending me for tests and, as they didn't know which specialist I needed, I was told I would be sent to both. Well I guess what they lied!

The gynaecology appointment had a 5 month waiting list so I was booked in for an appointment on May 29th, only to receive a letter 2 weeks before I was due to go to say that it'd been put back again another 2 months! Fuming as I was, I rang up and, after getting through to admin, I was told it was out of their hands because they'd had not 1, not 2, but 3 gynaecologists leave in the short space of a couple of months. I told the admin lady that this was far from my fault and that I'd already been waiting patiently for 5 months and she told me that other people are in the same situation.

Well guess what? I don't care about the other people right now; all I care about is me and my vagina. I mean how many people have hoo-hah issues right now?! Really! After stressing to the admin lady that my vagina was as important as anyone else's, I stupidly asked the wrong question of, "If I went private would I have this issue?" The answer was, "No, you'd be seen within 2 weeks!" F**k me. If I'd have known that 5 months ago, I would've gone private in the first place! I asked the admin lady who the best gynaecologist was to see, because my vagina issues were not going to last another 2 months and neither was my anxiety.

"Nuffield Health are your best bet but I don't know how much you'll be paying for a consultant." Now, I'd used Nuffield Health for spinal surgery and my gastric band, so I know they had a good reputation but when it came to my lady parts I was unsure. Another phone call to Nuffield Health put my mind at ease, even after having to talk to the poor fella about my foof issues to ensure I was directed to the right people. I was made aware that it would cost between £150-£250 for the consultation, which I was hoping that, because of a scheme I was with at work, they might have been able to help pay if further treatment was required. I didn't want just anyone poking around in my tuppence. And, yes I know I sound like a snob, but I wanted my issues sorting. I'd grown up being told that 'you always get what you pay for', which is kind of scary when you put that phrase in this context, but I stand by it.

My next hurdle was that they needed a letter from my GP's office. I was worried because if you go with the NHS, it takes around 2 months to be processed. But, low and behold, as soon as you say the word "private", it's the same day bloody delivery! This all happened on a Thursday. I received a phone call from Nuffield on the

Friday. And my confirmation letter came on the Saturday. If that's not super efficient, I don't know what is. There it was, all booked within 24hours, and under two weeks for my appointment. Boom! How easy was that?!

My only annoyance with the entire palaver was that the GP's should: 1. Tell me that there was an option to go private and that it would be quicker, especially when they know I was dealing with fertility problems; and 2. I was told I was going to see two specialists and only one referral was sent, unbeknownst to me. I just thought that there was a long waiting list for that specialist too. Nope, it turns out my referral wasn't even sent off! I know GP's see a lot of patient's day in, day out but, come on, it's not hard to send off a referral is it? Patience really was my bloody virtue here. And, I swear down, if I didn't have my hubby, and friends supporting me I would've been climbing the walls!

Here was to the 28th and hoping that most of my questions would be answered. Well a girl can hope, can't she?! Best get my razor sharpened to trim down the little garden I was growing. Although, I was quite getting used to it, much to the hubby's dismay.

An unfortunate tale of events

7 days into our two week wait, I'd started my pee on a stick addiction early and, as I stared down at that little white pee stick in anticipation, a very light shade of red hit the second line and stayed. There I was, sat on the toilet, not daring to move and thinking that I was seeing things. I also thought that I maybe needed to squeeze some more pee out for another stick. But no, there it was, that very faint, but very there second line. I certainly wasn't going to start singing and dancing about it all just in case.

Waiting another 2 days to take another test was just sheer hell. But I made it and the hubby nagged me to pee on a stick. There it was again, 9 DPO and the faintest of lines. It was no darker than the 2 days before so I really didn't have my hopes up and I told the hubby not to get his hopes up too. Until that special digital test gave me the word 'pregnant', I would not believe it. I told him that if I got to 14 DPO, I would pee on that special stick.

But that wasn't going to happen was it? As per the title, I peed on another stick, the same brand as the last two and it was negative. I was thinking "do I have a case of serious f*****g line eyes here?" But I couldn't have done because the hubby saw the second one and I'd sent a pic of the first one to a friend, who understood my situation. They'd confirmed I wasn't seeing things and even helped me tweak the test so I could see it better (inverted photo).

At 13 DPO, I started cramping and I noticed my temp on my very first BBT (basal body temperature) chart had dropped. And, low and behold, AF started. And boy did it flow (even the Mooncup couldn't handle it). Then came the cramps that were bad enough to make me sick, especially when the clots started coming thick and fast.

So, there I was, sitting on the toilet yet again wondering why? Why, when we slightly got our hopes up does life come and give you a swift kick in the vag to remind you; not this month sweetie - not this month; we were just kidding? Well f**k you hormones. I've had enough of this roller coaster called life.

Hopefully the gynaecologist could help me to understand why this kept happening. This was the 3rd time we'd had a suspected chemical pregnancy, with no reason as to why. For anyone not knowing what a chemical pregnancy is, it's basically a miscarriage before the 5th week. If I hadn't peed on sticks and got that faint positive, I would've just thought I was having a really bad period just like the other 2 times. The other two times I haven't told you about it because I didn't even know what was happening at the time.

The icing on the metaphorical cake

There I was, still bleeding, still feeling crappy and then, boom, my body kicked me when I was down. I got a cold, but not just any cold, I had a dose of acute pneumonia. What started with a cough got worse and worse until I was struggling for breath, and nearly passing out every time I coughed. I went to see my GP, who scared the beJesus out of me by sending me to hospital with a suspected blood clot in my lung. Just what I didn't need.

Getting to York hospital, I was directed to AMU (ambulatory care unit). I'd never been to this department before. But, luckily, I ended up having the best service that I've ever received from the NHS in that department. All the staff were friendly and caring and took their time helping me, which made me feel so much better.

After numerous tests I was told I had a chest infection with pleurisy. Although on my discharge papers, it stated pneumonia and hazy right lung x-ray. So it got me thinking: is pneumonia just a posh (doctor) word for saying chest infection now? I was given strong antibiotics and bed rest for a good week. Told to drink plenty of fluids as I hadn't been drinking enough water so I was dehydrated.

To summarise my shitty month.

So, to summarise my shitty month, my body was not a f*****g temple right then; it was a twat! On the plus side to this shit storm, I'd managed to lose another 4 pounds and only had 5 days to wait until I got to see the vajayjay inspector. There was only one way to go from that and that was hopefully up, up, up!

Keep on trucking

I was waiting patiently for yet another appointment, from yet another vajayjay inspector, with not much optimism on them actually helping me, as I'd not had much success with doctor's recently. Especially since most doctors just took one look at me and said to lose weight. They didn't take into any consideration how hard it is for someone with PCOS to actually lose weight and so you end up feeling like you're stuck in between a rock and a hard place.

Even with the gastric band, I'd lost weight but I was then stuck. It had plateaued off and it made me wonder whether I should have really had it done? Was it worth it? It was helping me maintain a healthy weight but that was partially because I wasn't enjoying food anymore. For instance, one day I thought I'd just grab beans on toast for lunch. Now, a normal adult portion before the band would have been two slices of toast and half a tin of baked beans. However, after the band, I could only manage half a slice of toast and about 6 tablespoons of baked beans before I was actually sick.

It kind of defeated the object when I had doctors telling me I wasn't losing weight because I wasn't eating enough. Then I had doctors telling me I was eating too much. So where does this criticism about weight and BMI ever end? It simply didn't. I felt like the doctors don't even see YOU; they just see you're overweight and that's that!

So, when my name was finally called forward, and I walked through into a little office room to have all my health checks done, I simply thought, "Here we go again, the dreaded scales. The one thing I hate more than not getting my own way!" "Take your shoes, and your jacket off, and step on the scales please Mrs Bone." For one, please don't call me Mrs Bone; it sounds so formal. And also, to me, there's only one Mrs Bone and that's the mother in law, "Just Kelly's fine thanks".

Also, why is it that in a doctor's office they use kilograms instead of stones and pounds like normal scales? So when you see the numbers hit the 90's all you think is "Shit! You big heffa!" I'm not great at maths so thank God for Google on this one, 94.3kg into stone please - 14st 8lb! I couldn't believe my eyes. I couldn't remember the last time the scales said under 15st, never mind nearly 14! I even queried it with the nurse as I didn't quite believe it. I have now concluded that my scales at home are wrong, so very wrong!

After having all my health checks done, I was led back into the waiting room for my official appointment. My nerves were starting to settle in and my stomach was growling, partially because it was approaching dinner time and I had forgotten to eat breakfast because I'd been rushing around trying to get ready and trying my hardest not to be late - I'm always late for everything. So bad, in fact, he set the clock forward in the kitchen. The last clock I look at before I leave, so, when I think I'm running late, technically I will be on time or sometimes even early.

I sat waiting and my appointment time came and went and, at this point, I was somewhat desperate for the loo but I knew it would just be my luck that if I went, my name would be called through. I felt like I had to chance it because if the vajayjay inspector actually had to investigate my vajayjay I wouldn't have liked to be uncomfortable. I was already uncomfortable enough after having to de-fluff the muff and it was now growing back. Well, you all know how that feels, like someone's just poured a million ants down one's panties. It's not a nice feeling. The things we do for beauty and floof appointments.

There I was, sat on the loo; yes, a nice image for you there, but that's where I was, and I could hear voices from the waiting room, and it was someone being called through; all I could think was, "I bloody knew it". It happens every time in the GPs' surgery. I nip to the loo and then I hear the machine go ping. I've never peed so quickly. Rushing back to the waiting room, it was empty; so after all that, it wasn't even my name that had been called forward.

When my name was finally called, I was led into a rather large clinical looking room and was asked to take a seat. I do, however, recall walking into the office and it smelling lovely, like the sweet smell of ladies' perfume. Sitting down, the consultant started off the conversation by introducing herself and then asked the question of "How can I help you?" This is the one question I always hate being asked as quite frankly I had so many questions to put forward that my mind went blank. I simply replied with, "Errrrm I'm not quite sure why I've been sent here". Now I did know why I had been sent there but it was that damn question. It put me right on the spot.

I then stumbled with the words "Well we're trying to conceive" and jabbered on about our past experiences with it and how we were doing it via artificial insemination due to the hospital turning us away because of my weight. This was still a very sore spot I'll tell you. After jabbering on for a good 10 minutes, I finally took a breath and let the doctor speak. Her reply was " Ok, so you've had X, Y, Z issues and you need my help in fixing them?" "YES, I need your help, please!"

The consultant's suggestions for my first initial problem of having 4 periods in one month and them being exceptionally heavy was to put me on the pill. But then knowing that we were trying for babies, that simply wasn't possible. After another quick chat about periods and heaviness etc., she told me that she was going to give me some medication to help slow the flow. "Brilliant", I thought. Only when she told me what the medication was, I had already tried that and it didn't work so she decided that we would tweak how I was to take it. How easy was that to sort out!

Secondly, during Round 4, we'd had another positive result, but then my period showed up yet again. This time, after researching chemical pregnancies, I was almost certain this is what we had had. The consultant confirmed this just by listening to what I was saying and then added that it's actually quite normal but most women don't realise it's happened. But, because I was avidly trying to conceive and watching and noting everything that was happening to my body, I was part of a minority that caught this. I spoke about how I don't ovulate all the time and again was told this was quite normal, especially in someone with PCOS. All I could think was, "Well I don't feel bloody normal."

Then, there it was, the whole speech I knew was coming, my weight. But instead of saying "You need to lose weight", she turned and looked directly into my eyes and said the words, "Well done, well done for how far you've come and what you've managed." It was at this point that the tears came rolling. I'd never been praised for what I'd accomplished. Usually I was told that it still wasn't good enough. But to hear those two simple words got to me.

It was at this point I knew that this consultant was willing to help me and hadn't just looked at me and thought "Well she's fat, that's why she's not getting anywhere." Yes, we did discuss my weight still being a hindrance, and she had suggestions, but I had literally tried every single one of them.

I then suggested that I had been on a medication a few years ago called Metformin which is usually used for diabetics, which I am not, but studies have shown that this medication combined with PCOS has had very positive results. When I first started taking it, I hadn't had a period for over a year and was desperate and so the Endocrinologist had prescribed it, and within a month or so, I was back to a regular 28 day cycle. Upon telling the consultant this, she agreed that I could try this again at a slightly higher dosage than before to see if it helped at all.

So, one appointment had completely given me a new outlook. It would take about 3 months for the medication to start working so we decided to have a break from trying to conceive until September time in order to give my body a chance to rest and catch up and for everything to settle back down.

Upon leaving the doctors office my face was adorned with a huge smile, knowing that within a few months my body could be back in sync, and more so, that I had finally been listened to and not criticised. Oh how I had waited for this moment. So until then, I would keep my head up high and keep on trucking.

A day in the life of a PCOS girl

Morning stretch, check. Morning fart, check. Ready to start my day full of beans and say hello to the world? Ha, yeah right if only. The only thing that was full of beans was my arse. I, however, was having to peel my eyelids open because, even after 8 hours of decent sleep, I was still tired, to the point that even my tiredness was tired.

Sliding out of bed, plodding into the bathroom, I casually caught a glimpse of myself in the mirror. Pass me the razor yet again as my facial fluff was back. I swear I can shave it all off and in an hour's time it would be sprouting back to life and, by the next day, I'm back to looking like sasquatch. Note to self: don't shave your face and then apply facial cream; it's a blotchy mess waiting to happen!

Where the hell did that zit come from? It was nowhere near rag week and there it was, Mount Fu**ing Vesuvius staring back at me. Baby arse cream to the rescue. I swear by this stuff. I have even been known to make a facemask out of it.

Heading downstairs with my belly growling at me, I was deciding whether I could eat another omelette yet again. It had kind of gotten boring now; maybe I would have to switch it up; maybe porridge, or Ready Brek? Yeah Ready Brek! Childhood memories at their finest.

First things first, I needed to see if the previous night's toilet time had made me lose a few pounds, as I hadn't been for a poo in over a week and my belly was starting to resemble a 6 month pregnancy belly. Low and behold, I had lost a pound; was that it for all that trouble? That pound would be back on again tomorrow, probably with another one added to it.

I made the dog's breakfast and nearly puked at the smell; how the f**k does he eat that shite?! The smell of it puts me off mine alone. Kettle boiled and morning brew was in the cup. I was still debating on whether I wanted breakfast. Even though I knew I needed to eat it, the new medication I was on made me feel somewhat nauseous in a morning. It also, however, needed to be taken with food to lessen the side effects, which defeated the object of it all!

Also, let me tell you, I seriously think it should be renamed Met-fart-min, never mind Metformin. It had gotten to the stage where I daren't let rip just in case it wasn't not safe. And I'd had a few of those occasions recently, not a nice experience when your toilet at work is down 2 flights of stairs!

Finally, I decided that a banana omelette it was. Probably not the greatest decision, but as I was currently competing with the hubby on who could lose the most weight before our holiday in two weeks, it was a wise decision. Breakfast scoffed and pots washed, I decided that I once again felt tired so decided the best thing I could do was to catch up on some pre recorded TV. And, it just so happened, that my guilty pleasure of Love

Island was recorded last night. Only, halfway through, I decided that I was too tired to actually take interest and so I cleaned the house instead, thinking that the exercise may help, especially when I was singing and dancing whilst dusting.

After cleaning for a good couple of hours and putting yet more washing in - I had no idea where it all came from as there were only two of us - I realised I had missed lunch. Since having the gastric band fitted, I sometimes did forget to eat, as I just wasn't hungry. And I know that if I ate at 15:30, and I would be having tea at 17:30, I would still be full, so I decided to skip it and wait. I needed to distract myself from thinking about food because, once I started to think about it, I started to become hungry and crave a sugar attack. Thankfully, I had thrown all the naughty treats away, except a rogue chocolate mini roll which just happened to fall into my mouth instead of the bin.

A distraction was needed desperately and so knitting came to my rescue. If I kept my hands busy, I would have no hands to eat food with. I did debate on taking the dog for a walk but with the rain almost imminent from the black cloud that had taken over the sky, he would have to wait. I spent a full hour knitting baby hats, for everyone except myself, telling myself that I really enjoyed it but that only worked for so long before the, "OMG they are just too cute took over", and that slight feeling of the green eyed monster came creeping in.

Thank God the hubby was home from work. Time to set aside the knitting and prepare tea, something I was meant to do earlier but ended up distracted by something else. Knives and forks at the ready to eat the most random of teas. It was the bizarre mix of fish fingers, chips, wedges, vegetable fingers (I kind of had a thing for these) and sweetcorn (only because the hubby likes to know how regular he is, as sweetcorn doesn't get digested). I must say here that, it was on this particular day, I was trying to run my freezer down so I could replenish it with healthy, diet foods, but of course, we needed to eat the naughty foods first.

Tea scoffed and belly's full, with that instant bloating as I'd eaten far too many high carb foods, it was time to be a couch potato and binge watch some random recorded programme yet again. It just so happened to be one of my favourites: Police Interceptors! Just as it was finishing, I realised I seriously needed a bath, as the smell I thought was coming from the dog, was actually coming from me!

I was having a nice long peaceful soak in the bath when I realised that I needed to wash my hair yet again, as you could cook chips in the grease coming off it. I wouldn't mind but I had literally only washed it the day before! Whilst shampooing up my hair, I caught another glimpse of myself in the mirror and thought to myself, "you goddamn hairy beast." It was back; the facial fluff was back. With added beard hair, just two stray ones sprouting out. They weren't there this morning! I gave up trying to pluck them and shaved the buggers off, knowing that if my bestie was here, she would be giving me the, "You shouldn't shave" speech "As it will grow back thicker." I knew this and yet I still had not learnt the lesson.

After all that, I was so tired I knew it was bedtime for me. Even though it was only 9pm, I was done. Pyjamas and eye mask adorned, and ear plugs at the ready. Relax. That was until a little thing called insomnia kicked in and I saw every goddamn hour until about 2am. Then it was morning once again.

I needed a break

When you're at that point in your journey and you just think Fu*k this shit, I've had enough. Even though I'd had positive results from the gynaecologist and was put on the correct medication, I felt physically and emotionally drained, to the point where I thought I really need to heed some advice and take a break, not just from trying to conceive, but from reality. Our little holiday couldn't come quick enough.

I was just hoping that this period I was having was going to be over, as by God it was the period from hell. I wasn't sure if it was all my new medication kicking in or whether it was just a really bad period. It was the type where you're sitting on the toilet not knowing if you're going to puke, shit or if your uterus was going to fall out of your vagina. The pain was coming in waves every 5 minutes. And it was at that point that I thought, "Oh my God, this better not be what labour feels like because, if it is, I may have to rethink this whole baby thing over." It was excruciating. As the pain ripped through me, I couldn't help but cry, shake and wail like a banshee, hoping that I wouldn't be one of those clichéd women who didn't know that they were pregnant until the baby plopped out into the toilet.

Plop. What the fu*k was that? That my dears was a clot the size of my palm landing in the depth of the toilet bowl! It was at that point the hubby popped his head around the door and asked if I was okay. "DO I LOOK LIKE I'M OKAY?" I said through gritted teeth. He asked me if he needed me to call someone and I replied with, "Who are you going to call? If you say Ghostbusters, I will kill you!" Now was not the time for a sense of humour. I proceeded to tell him that I needed strong painkillers. But as I kept throwing up, they wouldn't get in my system. This was the cue for him to remember that when I'd had my gastric band fitted I'd been given liquid painkillers. Perfect. I was hoping that he'd hurry as I couldn't take much more of the pain. I'd been sat on the loo, clutching the bin in one hand and my stomach in the other, for over an hour, to the point I literally couldn't feel my legs and my arse was firmly stuck to the pot!

10 mins later, the pain was going down from a 9 to a 2. I could still feel it but at least now it was manageable and I could unpeel my arse from the toilet seat! After an hour of that, I was exhausted and needed a nanna nap. Even though I knew we were supposed to be setting off for Durham, as it was our eldest niece's 18th birthday - man, that made me feel old - but I just couldn't, not just yet. The hubby told me to have a quick snooze then we'd set off a bit later.

An hour or so later, I woke up feeling so much better, like it was all a dream. Only the bathroom told me a different story as it resembled something out of a horror movie. A quick shower, face on and I was ready to face the world again. I wasn't going to let period pain stop me from getting on with my life. Also, we were going on holiday the next day, so I had to just crack on with it.

On the way up to Durham, we made the decision to book an overnight hotel because we were both shattered and it wouldn't make sense to drive all the way home to then drive back again in a few hours. It was lucky we did that because, after we'd spent time with the family, it was getting late and we knew we had to be up early. 4am early! Alarms set and we were ready.

I was awoken to two different alarms, not knowing which one to hit first. The hubby however was still fast asleep, snoring his little head off, until the hotel room started to ring. Upon answering it, in his half-sleep state, he managed to drop the receiver, mumbling the words "Thanks." I facepalmed myself whilst saying to him, "Wake up, wake up you've dropped the phone." "What?" "The phone, the phone you've dropped it." He wasn't very good at waking up in the morning. Can you tell?

Phone call sorted, make up plastered on my face, and hair flight-selfie ready, it was go, go, go. I think I was more excited that I could actually catch some zzz's when we got on the plane. Although that didn't happen. I'd just made myself comfy: hood over my eyes and my arms tucked into the opposite sleeves, I was sleep ready. Until the little brats in front of me started shouting and making a pest out of themselves. Now, I know kids get excited, but 2 hours worth of that? I could not survive!

Earplugs were firmly placed in my ears and I was off again. But not for long. I kept feeling something tickling my foot. I thought it must've been the air hostesses trolley. But, when it kept going on, I peeled off my hood from my eyes to find some little twat standing on my feet. After a swift boot and a long glare, he buggered off back to his seat. He knew what he was doing but kept doing it anyway! My hubby said that he'd been woken up to the same kid stroking his leg, seriously? Fecking weird child!

I was so glad that we were going to an adult only hotel because, as much as I love kids, they can be arseholes! Then suddenly it dawned on me that next year we could be coming away with our child. I know I was wishful thinking, but I couldn't help it. We can all dream can't we? Hopefully that dream would one day become a reality.

Rant Alert

Why is it so hard for people to talk about infertility or even just fertility issues in general? I know it's not like I go around wearing a huge t-shirt with the words "talk infertility to me", but I'm very much an open book and, if you ask the questions, I will answer. Stop letting it be an elephant in the room!

Take the other day for example, I bumped into someone I hadn't seen for years. They knew I was married and asked, "So when are you having kids then?" Now, I wasn't going to answer that question with a lie because I didn't see why I should be embarrassed about our issues. I answered with "It's taking us longer as we have issues". Their answer? "Sorry". Really, seriously! I didn't say that for pity. I said it because it was true. *Sorry* was not the answer I was expecting.

So, here's a general rule for you, if you so happen to have word vomit and like to ask couples when they are popping out sprogs, and they say they're having issues, don't f*****g reply with sorry! That actually made me angry for the rest of the day. I actually didn't know what to say back. Also, why do people think that just because we were struggling ourselves that meant that we couldn't be happy for other people?

I'm sick of reading statuses on social media groups about how they've had a clear out of friends because they were pregnant before them. What is wrong with people?! Yes, there's that little pang of jealousy, and sometimes a bit of pain to go with it, but seriously, de-friending someone because they got pregnant and you didn't? Grow the f**k up!

Of course, it's difficult to see an old friend on her fourth or fifth child but I can still be happy for them and congratulate them. I wouldn't delete her just because she has something that I don't. My thought was that my time would come and I know that that person will be as happy for me as I was for them. I know a lot of people who are reading this will say that I'm being too hard but I was in that situation. I know how hard it is. But if we deleted every single pregnant person or people with children from our lives, we would have no friends left.

I must admit, the one thing that really does get on my last nerve is people who are sitting at their keyboards talking about how shit their pregnancy is, or how they wish it would just hurry up. They're the type of people that piss me right off. They don't know what they actually have. They should embrace it, not sit there f*****g whinging about it. They're the type of people who I would understand if you delete them.

And then, another thing, you've got Betty over there saying how shit her life is because she's had kids one after the other and now can't cope. That one in my eyes is simple: STOP and take a look at what you have Betty and be f*****g grateful about it. There's people out there that would give anything to be in your shoes. Also, your kids are little shits because you let them be. It's that simple. Rant over.

The fear is real

What if it fails? What if we have another chemical? What if we have to look into other options? What if, what if, what if... My follow up appointment had come through for the private gynaecologist and it was for the 27th August. I was actually looking forward to it.

The consultant I'd seen the previous time was lovely and so helpful. I was hoping she'd be able to work her magic once more as I had a slight problem. I'd been taking the medication she prescribed to try to regulate my periods again properly and I think I got a bit too excited. It worked the first time. I was now thinking that it was a fluke.

Let's talk about periods yet again. My first period, after starting my medication was the one, I thought I was dying and I was NOT being dramatic either. After that horrendous time, I actually had normal (well what I assume to be normal) ovulation on CD (cycle day) 16. On average, most women ovulate on or around CD14. So this is where I got a little bit too excited too prematurely because Mr Blobby popped up on CD28 which was amazing. I hadn't had a normal cycle for so long.

But here's the big but: I didn't ovulate the next month until CD21. Originally I thought I'd ovulated on CD18, which I would have accepted, but nope I was wrong - which I can't believe I'm actually admitting! The worst thing about this cycle was that it was another long one and Aunt Flow didn't show up to spoil the party until CD33! Some shitty aunt she was. I always thought aunts were meant to be nice. But, oh no, not this one; this one was one mean mother fluffer.

I think the only upside to it was that they weren't as heavy anymore. (TMI alert). Before the doctor's, and before her giving me the meds, I used to fill a Mooncup every hour. That's nearly 80ml every hour for the first 2 days! Then it would just trickle for what I would assume would be a normal monthly for another 5 days. Yes, 1 week of the month. Avoid this woman. She turns into a mean, hormonal mother fluffer!

If you're wondering why my swearing has somewhat calmed down, we had the pleasure of having our 12 year old niece stay over for the weekend and I refused to drop the 'big' swears in front of her. No child should hear them. Although, most of them already know them before they're 6 years old! So, she taught me to say "fluff" instead of "f**k" and it had stuck. I actually quite liked it. I'd rather be called a "mother fluffer" any day!

Right, getting back to it, my fandango inspection was fast approaching and I just hoped she would just be able to say that, as I had a normalish cycle the first time, that she could just tweak the meds to make me, or at least my periods, normal again. Boy what I would've given to be regular and clockwork so I could actually mark my calendar with a big red splodge and not have to move it every damn month!

After I'd been to see the specialist, we should've known then if we were good to start trying for babies again and I could release this chastity belt and hang my 'open' sign up once more. Even though we wouldn't be trying again until the October/ November cycle due to the fact I was going on holiday.

Me and the bestie decided that we would tick something off our bucket lists before I had babies. We were going to Iceland and I know that, even though it's only a short flight, I wasn't willing to risk it. We would get back in late September so, all being well with my cycle, we would be able to start gearing up ready to go in October.

That's if the flights hadn't made my body weird again. It happens every time I fly. I either get my period late or not at all. I'm not too sure as to why, but flying does some weird things to my body. Mainly it makes me expand and fills me full of wind - which is not a nice feeling and I don't like letting it out on flights because I hate the thought of people breathing in my farts for 2hours. I think the hubby would agree on that one!

As the baby making was fast approaching, the fear was getting very real and my anxiety around it was too, especially after last time; getting excited, even though I knew I shouldn't have, all for it to be taken away a few days later. But, what doesn't kill you makes us stronger - or so the saying goes. So we would have to just wait and see. That was the hard part. The wait was what I hated the most. And, don't even get me started on the two week wait again, 3 days into that and I'm always telling it to kiss my arse because I just want to know!

We only had 2 more months to wait. What was two months eh? When you'd been waiting for years for anything to happen. As I'd always been told, good things come to those who wait.

Here we go again

I bought a diary. It wasn't anything fancy; just your normal bog-standard 2019/2020 lined diary. Only, I wasn't going to be using it as a normal diary. It was going to be full of pee sticks, starting the next month, when my full blown POAS addiction would surely kick in again. I was ready for round errrrrrm, I couldn't actually remember what round we were going to be on that time. It felt like it had been that long!

Although I felt I definitely needed the break. It had given me the chance to lose some more chunk and my medication chance to work it's magic. It was currently CD 15 and I was having that delightful EWCM, which everyone loves. Not! The only good thing about having that squelch plopping out of your vajayjay is that you either know to have copious amounts of nookie, if you're trying for babies, or for us it was turkey baster time. So for all you ladies not trying to conceive, that snot-looking white gunk means that the chastity belt needs to be firmly put in place. There is no excuse for 'accidents'. You have been warned.

CD 18 and the egg had been released and boy did I feel that one. All I can say is that I was glad my body was finally sorting its own issues out and that I was ovulating roughly on time, give or take a few days. I'll take those few days anytime though rather than a week before my period was due. At least when we did try again later in the year, well what was left of it, it should've been all systems go, go, go!

I had one last hurdle to overcome before we could try again though. And that meant yet another doctor. I was beginning to think that I was some kind of hypochondriac. I was having some issues with my gastric band, to the point I couldn't eat. Literally every meal I ate, I enjoyed it that much that I got to taste it two or three times more. Gross, I know. But if you've read this far, you'll know by now I don't hold back!

So I had to go to the hospital to have some fluid released from the band so I could eat properly. The only issue I had was that the doctor couldn't find the port; it was hiding somewhere in my body, which in turn meant that I needed it done under x-ray guidance. That said, I left the appointment thinking all sorts of weird things about where my port could be including, "Had my stomach eaten it as it was that hungry?" or "Have I pooped it out just thinking it was a rather large turd?" I mean, come on. How can you lose a port in your body? The doc didn't exactly give me answers. They never do. I only knew that it was being difficult. My appointment was booked for two weeks' time, which was great as it meant that, hopefully, I would be able to eat normal people food when I went to Iceland with my bestie the week after.

Two weeks passed rather quickly and I was sat waiting to have my X-ray to see where my port was hiding. The nurse approached me, with her clipboard in hand, asking me the general questions: name, address etc and then, there it was, "Is there any chance you could be pregnant?" To which I replied with, "definitely not!" "Ah ok, so why do you say that?" All I really wanted to say was that it was none of her goddamn business, and to just take my word for it, but I settled for, "Because we can't have children naturally and we aren't currently trying at the minute." The nurse turned and said, "I'm really sorry, I have to ask these things?" Personally, I think if you say there's no chance you could be pregnant, and sign a waiver, then there's no reason for them to ask why!

X-rays done and I found out I hadn't pooped it out. It had just sunk further in so he needed a longer needle. But job's a good un. I was all sorted and I was ready to eat me some normal people food instead of mush.

Now my band was all fixed, and I had the green light from the vagina inspector that, once the next period happened, I could start tracking once again. Peeing on more sticks, oh how I'd missed doing that; it had become part of my routine! Fingers crossed that 2020 would be our year for babies, or baby, I wasn't greedy.

Bucket list before babies?

As I knew we were taking a break from baby making for a while, back in June I'd decided I needed a holiday, nothing extravagant just a little weekend away somewhere. So, me and the bestie had decided to book a trip to Iceland. It's one of those places that's on most people's bucket list, especially to see the Northern Lights and to swim in the Blue Lagoon. That was that. We both looked at each other and said "F**k it, lets just book it! Let's do this!" It would be a once in a lifetime opportunity and I couldn't wait to share the experience with Sarah.

I did, however, have one thing on my mind as we were booking it: me and the hubby had said that we would try for babies again come September but that was the only time I could get off work. So baby making would just have to be put on hold for a bit longer so I could tick this from my bucket list because I don't suppose it's somewhere you would think to take a child. Also, I didn't want to risk flying incase we did fall pregnant. So much stress and planning goes into something so small. The worry that comes with it comes in abundance.

Decision made, depending upon if my periods weren't having a 'moment': the baby making would be put on hold an extra month to give me time to tick this one last thing from my bucket list before babies came along. The countdown was on for both the holiday and baby making. I didn't know which one I was more excited for!

2 more sleeps to go, which in turn meant two more nights shifts for me because I couldn't get the extra days off from work. So, like an idiot, I thought I'd be fine with a power nap and copious amounts of coffee. How wrong I was. Unpacking and packing my suitcase for the fifth time, I kept thinking "Oh god I've forgotten something" and then I remembered something the hubby always says to me when I go on my pre holiday packing rant: "I'm sure they have shops abroad, you know." I know he's right - not that I'd ever let him know that though. So, I came to the conclusion to heed his advice, and go "F**k it" whatever I've forgotten I'll just buy out there. As long as I had clean knickers and socks, I was good!

Upon finishing my nightshift, I raced home but realised I didn't have enough time to wash my hair. Ah, no one was going to notice my bed head; they were all going to be too excited. Quick shower, minus the hair wash, and face slapped in makeup to hide the somewhat sleep-deprived looking eyes and I was ready. *Passports, check; money, check; phone and charger, no check - oh god where had I put them? I couldn't ring it; it was on silent. Shit! F**k! Had I left them at work? No, Kelly, retrace your footsteps. You came in from work and had your pre-flight poo. Ah! The bathroom, where I was playing some shite game whilst sat on the loo? Nope, not in the bathroom. Oh god I had 5 mins until me mam arrived to take us. Where the hell had I put them?* After 2 mins pacing and searching, I eventually found them right where I'd left them to remind myself not to forget them - in my coat pocket. I mean, where else would they be?!

That drama over and a quick once over of my bag, we were in the car heading for the train station. I'd never caught the train to the airport before so my anxiety was a little bit higher than normal, especially after a dream I'd had where the train got stuck and we missed our flight. It turned out that dream may have represented reality. As the train pulled into Manchester Victoria, there was an announcement over the tannoy announcement stating: "This train will terminate here due to a bomb threat at Manchester airport." My jaw couldn't have dropped any further upon hearing this and my mouth went dry. Me and Sarah both looked at each other and said, "What the hell do we do now?!"

It was 1hr 30mins to get to the airport in time for boarding. There were no taxis, buses or trams. Arrrrrgh, this wasn't happening. After a painful 15mins, we found a taxi who would take us for £30 - the robbing bastards! The airport was on the horizon and so was the queue of traffic. The taxi driver turned to us and said we would have to walk quite a bit of the way (he still wanted £30 though).

With 30 mins to get there, there was no way we were making that flight but I'd be damned if I wasn't going to try! I turned to Sarah and said, "We are on a mission, let's do this, just keep up." We had at least a 20min walk ahead of us just to get to the terminal. But by some miracle we made it, albeit sweaty as hell, but we even made it with time to spare. Even security was pretty quick for once despite a bomb scare nearby!

There was a quick stop at Boots for the much needed forgotten items and we were finally boarding. Iceland here we came. After a 2hr flight sitting next to a stranger who couldn't stop talking about themselves and how successful their life was and how much money they were making and the cars and boats they owned, I was ready to get out of that plane. All I wanted to do was say that "nobody cares" but instead I chose to humour him and made it my entertainment for the flight. I have no idea whether it was his weird chat up line or what? Although, he was supposed to be getting married soon. Good luck to his wife to be eh! Let's just say it humoured me for two hours at least.

The first impression of Iceland I have is being at the back of a bus fast asleep catching flies. I was beat; the night shifts finally caught up with me. The bus that was supposed to take us directly to our hotel dropped us off in, what can only be described as, the middle of nowhere with a finger point to say "Hotel down there." Cheers mate! The 'hotel down there' turned into a 5 minute walk down a hill with Google maps trying to direct us.

We made it and were pleased to be able to get checked in. The hotel reminded me of walking through the bedroom section of Ikea. It even had the same woody smell to it. Andddd relax. Bag unpacked, thermals adorned; it was time to get this adventure started.

Firstly, I needed food as my belly was growling as if it was angry at me. We walked and walked, and walked some more and then, there it was, the red and black sign that was such a familiar sight: The Hard Rock Cafe! With our stomachs full, we decided to walk some more before calling it a night. We popped in and out of little, what I like to call, "shitty shatty shops", as literally they were just full of tourist shite. But right in the middle of them all was the best shop ever; the Christmas shop. If I see a Christmas store, 'I have a big smile'! Directly opposite that Christmas store was a Tourist Information Centre which was actually open. We came out of there £200 lighter and that was only for one trip, which we were so excited to go on the next day.

Waking up the next day, I was excited that I was finally ticking that place off my bucket list: The Blue Lagoon. That was where we were going to spend the day and, let me tell you, it didn't disappoint. The serene atmosphere, the gentle warm water and the amazing views. The only problem that I had was that that was also the day Aunt Flow had decided she was really angry at my uterus and kept giving me really bad period cramps. And, towards the end of the day, it had defeated me to the point that painkillers had firmly been brought into action. It didn't put too much of a damper on the day though. It just meant I was constantly asking Sarah to check my arse to see if I was leaking anywhere, as my swimsuit was green. Even after heavily debating whether or not to pack the black one, I'd decided on green. Always go with your gut instinct, they say don't they. This was why! Shrivelled like prunes, we called it a day at 4pm, knowing that if we got back in time, we might have had the chance to catch the boat to explore the night skies for the Northern Lights. Arriving back from the Blue Lagoon at about 6pm, we knew we were pushing it to make it for the Northern Lights but we had to try.

And, we were in luck. The boat wasn't sailing that evening until 11pm, which meant we had time to get changed and have a quick Mugshot, aka Mac and Cheese in a mug, before walking yet again to the marina in order to set sail into the night. We didn't have much luck seeing anything really, other than a white smear in the dark sky, which quite frankly could've been a cloud to the naked eye. If you had a special camera filter, you could see the green colours but unfortunately neither me nor Sarah had that capability on our phones. Or so we thought.

The next night I was determined to see the lights so I found a light filter app on my camera settings. But after standing outside for over an hour and no luck, I was about to give in when I decided to shout up to the sky, "Come on grandma, show us the lights please?" Just like that, my camera started to focus and a green smear appeared in the open clouds. There it was. Our Northern Lights sighting. Ever so slight but it was there. It wasn't until I had fully captured it on my camera, and we zoomed in, that we both could see a baby's face in the green light. At first it was hard to make out but there it was. I couldn't help but hope so I made a wish there and then, hoping that with Round 5 fast approaching it would be a happy one.

Everybody hurts sometimes

A psychiatrist once told me that if you can't say words out loud, then write them down to get them off your mind. I was currently 2 DPO after finishing Round 5 and I felt like I was back on that emotional rollercoaster again and I just wanted to get off. Whoever said trying for babies is easy, was definitely telling porky pies. It's the most stressful thing I've ever done.

I managed to get insemination done the day before, and the day of my ovulation but then, due to my shift work pattern, we couldn't get any done in the lead up because I was working 12 hour days. Cue me panicking that it may not be enough and consulting Dr Google to reassure myself. Obviously, Google helped ease my anxiety. But, I mean, some people have sex just once and, hey presto, like magic, they're pregnant. Slightly different for us I know, as we had to plan every last little detail, even down to keeping a specimen pot in my handbag. I could imagine that falling out when I don't want it to. Although, I don't think it would be as embarrassing as the time I went to the bank counter with an envelope full of money with the words 'spunk fund' written on it in bright pink highlighter. Now that was embarrassing. I had the hubby's sense of humour to blame for that one.

Back to the story. I mean rant. We'd just had an amazing weekend away in Harrogate. It was just what we both needed some hubby and wifey time. On the way home, I was hit by extreme tiredness, which took me aback as I'd had a good night's sleep and I'd rested. But damn that 20min power nap just had to be done. Waking up feeling refreshed, we decided to clear out the garage, something that we'd needed to do for so long but neither of us could be arsed. It was a big job and something I wish we'd never started. 2 hours later, it was finished and if I could cartwheel that's what I would've done on the nice clean floor. But, as I can't, I just admired our handy work from the door; in my head, I was doing said cartwheel.

After that, I was ready just to chill out on the sofa in my onesie with a brew, a decaf brew of course, because I don't want to not be able to sleep. I was sitting on the sofa, debating what takeaway we should get: would it be an Indian or pizza? But as it was only 4pm, no takeaway was open cue me getting my pout on. I really fancied an Indian but I couldn't wait another 2 hours for one to open. I also couldn't be arsed to cook as that tiredness from earlier had smacked me in the face again so I decided to just throw a pizza in the oven. Although, I was in a mood with myself because I didn't want pizza! I decided that I would have garlic bread with extra garlic to make me think it was a naan bread; although, I regretted that decision later on as, not only did I stink, it kept repeating on me all night. Finally, I sat down on the sofa for the night: garlic bread to the left of me, and naughties to the right (naughties are what me and the hubby call sweets, chocolate, popcorn, anything naughty and edible really).

They were sat patiently, waiting to be eaten with the movie - that we never ended up watching. Flicking through all the shite we'd recorded through the week, we found one of our favourite detective series and agreed to watch that. This is where it all started.

A couple of episodes in, and the gay guys had decided they were going to adopt. I was totally fine with this until the thoughts started creeping into my head of "What if we have to adopt?" I literally don't think I could do it. So that set me off emotionally. Silently crying to myself, wishing the program to be over so I could just stop thinking. I tried to escape by logging onto social media to find not one, not two, but three baby scan pictures which added to it all. As I've said before, I can be happy for them but sometimes and some days, like then, I just couldn't deal with it. My emotions were far too high.

The push too far was when I took myself to the kitchen to breathe and the hubby came in with a million and one questions that I couldn't handle. All I could say was that he didn't understand how I was feeling right now, even though I knew he did, and I just needed 5 minutes to compose myself. But he couldn't give me that, which made me snap and take my frustration out on him. It's hard to explain how you're feeling when you feel so alone sometimes. I know why I was feeling so hurt but, right then, I wasn't ready to say it out loud. Right then, all I needed to do was cry, shout and let it all out. Instead

I calmly took myself to the bathroom and sobbed my little heart out alone.

Once I'd finished having the little tantrum with myself, I heaved myself downstairs and was greeted with a big hug, which set off the ugly cry once again and, anyone who knows me, knows I don't cry. If you've ever seen me cry, you're a very privileged person! I sat down to watch the end of the programme that, even with all the emotional bits, I was actually thoroughly enjoying. I couldn't help but think why the hell am I so emotional and tired?

The next day I needed a rant as still I hadn't escaped the gloomy feeling and knew I had to off load. So, a quick phone call to my bestie, and she was around within an hour with a big squishy hug, the type of hugs that I would usually give to people when they are feeling like shite. A brew, some crumpets, and a good hour putting the world to rights later, I felt like my load was lifted and dumped straight into the toilet. I know it's okay to hurt because everybody hurts sometimes.

Well this just sucks.

Well this just sucked. How did I know my body was a female? Because it liked to f**k with me and, once it was done, it just spat me back out into the world without two shits to give.

Round 5 was officially in the vagina and it was into the TWW. The TWW is something I definitely hadn't missed whilst on our break. Everyday you're on countdown until you can piss on the sticks. I happened to resist pissing on the sticks until 7 DPO, and the only reason why I did was because I woke up with a wave of nausea sweeping through my body. Sat on the toilet waiting for another stick to tell me that it's not this month when a shade of pink swept over the test line - so faint I could only just see it. But it was there. It was there enough for me to be able to capture it with my phone's camera.

8 DPO and there was still a very, very faint line so I wasn't getting my hopes up as, after 3 chemicals, I'd started to think my body wasn't cut out for babies.

9 DPO and still with early morning pee, there it was again: the smallest, faintest pink line. This was the day I was going on a night out with my 18 year old niece and my bestie. This was the night I'd been looking forward to for months. The night I could finally get to show the niece how it was done. I didn't expect to be on mocktails all night.

As we got in from our 5 hour shopping trip to Leeds, I was busting yet again for another pee so I thought, "Right I'm going to rule this can I, can't I drink whilst I'm out." So as I jumped in the bath to soak my aching feet, the pee stick nicely draining on some loo roll on the window sill, I psyched myself up for it to come back negative. And that would be fine. A positive would be a bonus but a negative would also be accepted due to the test line in the others being so faint. After daydreaming for a few minutes, the pee stick timer went off and, wait: what?! It was a dark prominent test line. Oh my days. Was this it? Was it my turn to finally say the words, "I'm pregnant"?! Soaking deeper in my bath smiling to myself, I knew I had to save the news for the next day after the niece had gone home. Going out on the night out, and knowing that I couldn't say a word, was hard but somehow I managed to control myself.

The night out

After the shock had settled down, we needed to get ready. Now, us girls take at least 2 hours to prepare ourselves for a night out and that's if we're rushing too. We have to contemplate what outfit will go with what shoes and then whether we can actually walk in those shoes. We have to make sure that the handbag then goes with the outfit - not that anyone's paying any attention to the accessories, or the necklace that was now dangling in between the ample bosom which was currently spilling from my jumpsuit. I decided that the necklace was far too much and would just end up annoying the shit out of me so back in the drawer it went.

Next, onto the makeup because makeup must be done before the hair. Also with makeup, when we're going out out, it must be plastered on so as not to budge and with highlighter applied liberally. The finishing touch to any makeup would usually be copious amounts of hairspray to try and stop it running down my face by the end of the night, but on the earlier shopping trip I'd decided to treat myself to a £10 bottle of magic spray. It claims not to let makeup budge all night and said it wouldn't leave me looking oily; let's just say, the way I dance, I didn't have high hopes for it actually doing its job!

Makeup done. The hair was now ready to be back combed into a hairstyle that Amy Winehouse would be proud of. The sort of hairstyle that looks awesome when you start the night and then somewhat resembles the style of getting dragged through a bush backwards by the end of it.

After getting myself ready, the niece was admiring my eyeshadow handy work so I ended up doing her makeup too. I thought I liked glitter but, after applying a small amount thinking that would be ample on the niece, I was met with 'more'. Well she asked for it so of course I obliged. Only, because it was so fine, it got bloody everywhere and, no matter how hard you wiped it off, you just ended up spreading it around.

With Alexis now looking like a glitter princess, with makeup that even wowed me, despite the fact that I did it, it was time for her hair. We decided to do a bit of 'twinning' and have matching hair as well as makeup. I was game for that, wanting to live up to the 'cool auntie' name.

All ready and the countdown was on, we just needed Sarah. 8pm came and went and then I started getting the nervous stomach. You all know what that means. Let's just say the toilet seat was rather warm when I'd finished, as the flush eliminated my worries. I heard the front door go and in walked Sarah and, when I saw her, my mouth fell to the floor. I'd only seen her a few days prior and she was a shoulder length blonde. Now in walked this short bobbed redhead. I think my words were "Oh my god, your hair". I did happen to tell her it looked lovely eventually, after getting over the change. Selfies taken and then we were on our way to hitting the town.

Excitement was buzzing around the car. Me and Sarah were still trying to adapt to Chloe's (who changed her name to Alexis) name. I had known her as Chloe for 6 nearly 7 years and to try and then call her something new was so hard; I think I somehow managed it towards the end of her stay.

Tottering up to the bar of choice with teeth chattering and nipples that could cut glass, I was pleased to see there was no queue and, for just one moment, I got excited as I heard the words, "Have you got ID please?" I thought "Whoop, whoop I've still got it", until I realised he was actually asking my niece!

Heading to the bar I had a weird feeling in my stomach as I pondered whether I should drink or not. As quickly as the thoughts came into my head, the words, "Pink gin and lemonade" came out of my mouth, I mean the odd drink wasn't going to do much harm as I still wasn't 100% sure if there was a bun in the oven.

We were soon all sitting at the table sipping on our drinks, people watching and singing along to the cheesy music that was being blasted into our ears, before I found the cocktail menu. I thought that if we shared a big one at least then they wouldn't know how much I was or wasn't drinking. Sarah came back from the bar with, what can only be described as, a giant martini glass full of ice and some purple drink sloshing around it. It did, however, taste better than it looked.

After numerous daft selfies and the giant cocktail demolished, we decided it was time to head to Church - not to declare our sins - but for yet more cocktails (or a mocktail for me) and a good boogie on the dancefloor. Well, that was until we realised you could barely move, not because it was busy, but the fact that the floor was so sticky you literally had to shuffle your feet to move. It got to the point where we couldn't enjoy the dancefloor,so we moved on to good old Popworld: full of old people, hen do's and cheesy music.

The best thing about not being drunk is the fact you get to laugh at everyone else acting like total twats. The worst thing about not being drunk is I could feel my feet aching; I was tired; and I could've easily curled up in the corner. I knew it was getting to cheesy chips time and then bedtime.

Chips paid for, we stood waiting patiently and then our entertainment for the night walked in, in the form of some girls that were so wankered they could barely walk, never mind stand. One hit the deck, taking her chips with her, along with a pot of garlic mayonnaise which she was now wearing, all down her lovely black dress. But she had no shits to give; all she wanted was her food.

After our little bit of evening entertainment left, we started the slow walk to the taxi rank where we were getting picked up from. At that point, I knew I'd eaten too quickly, forgetting that chips got stuck in my band.

Luckily I still had the box they had come in as I was saving the rest for the hubby; only he wasn't going to get the chance to eat any because I liked mine that much that I got to see them twice. As it was literally just saliva and a chip, it wasn't like normal sick; it was like a long stringy bogey. But, as it was stretchy, what I thought I had caught in the chip box, was now dangling down my cleavage. How not to end your night: needing your friend to hunt through bags for tissues to shove down your sick tits. Bedtime.

The day after, the night before

So, back to the fact I'd had a positive test the previous night. I thought I'd surprise the hubby with a fresh one. Only, staring back at me were the painstaking words 'NOT PREGNANT'. What? How was that even possible? I knew I was only approximately 10 DPO but I knew people who'd gotten their BFP's around here. As we still had the niece with us, I couldn't find it in myself to mope around about it and I had to stick that happy smile back on my face, even though inside I was ugly crying.

I had promised the hubby earlier on in the week that Sunday was pee on a stick day but how was I going to tell him this? And crush him yet again? Even he'd been convinced I was pregnant this time. But that digital test with its shouty capital f**k you said it all, didn't it? I know we weren't officially out until The Witch turned up but I was half expecting her to show right on time on Thursday. So, was this another chemical in the bag? Or was it simply faulty piss sticks? 5 of them to be precise. F**k knows. All I knew is, I was sick of this shit.

The 5 stages.

I should've been used to this: getting my hopes up only for them to be squashed a few days later. Round 5 was a success. Well, it was for a few days, before my body decided that it didn't want to be pregnant. And with one swift kick in the vag, The Witch had made me bleed again.

I didn't even get to pee on my shiny new First Response pee stick on the Thursday because, on the Tuesday, I started cramping really badly, to the point that it woke me up in the middle of the night. But there was no bleeding at that point. So, here was me, sat on the toilet, stupidly thinking I still had a chance. After our other chemicals, you would think that I would have realised that this was just all in my head. The cramps were that bad that they made me sick - which was not normal! Not for me anyway. I felt like I was in the first stage of grief - utter denial. Denial that it was actually happening and that within a few hours, I would be bleeding like a bitch.

Low and behold, a few hours later, it started to flow. As the pain swept through me, I was struggling for breath. Stage 2. Now I was angry that this was happening again. I loathed my body for putting me through this pain and anguish. I was willing it all to disappear. I somehow missed out stage three as nothing I said to my body or myself was going to bring back what once was - even if it was only for a day.

Crawling back into bed with the duvet over my head, I begged the day to be over as, quite frankly, it could go fuck itself! I sat looking through my phone, torturing myself by looking at the pictures of each positive test. Silently I was sobbing to myself that it all must've been in my head and I had line eyes. Only it wasn't. The hubby had seen them too. I felt racked with guilt. I questioned myself as to why I even showed him as I'd vowed I wouldn't until that digital read the words 'pregnant' and I had even devised an exciting way of telling him. But all that changed when I saw that positive test on the Saturday afternoon. The next morning, I'd not even been able to contain myself as he asked me if I'd peed on a stick yet and I'd just said "Come see".

The diary that once contained all my little green ovulation pee sticks was now on a page with little blue pregnancy sticks, each with a faint yet visible line staring back at us and then, there was Saturday afternoon's, blazing red second line. I had always told myself that I wouldn't get my hopes up just in case. But right then my heart took over from my brain as I'd imagined that in 9 months' time, we could be parents.

When you long for something so bad, I think you can almost mindfuck yourself into thinking it's real. Back from the daydream, I was realising that maybe my body just wasn't cut out for babies or maybe I wasn't meant to be a mammy?! I was trying to reason with myself that it's a normal process as that's what the doctors had told me: if we have a chemical, it's just your body getting rid of a nonviable pregnancy. When I first heard of a chemical, I thought that's what they called it, if you longed for something that much, that your own will power could change the colour of the pregnancy test. I have since found out that that is a load of shit. You can only get a second line if the pregnancy hormone is in your body. So, it wasn't in my head after all?!

Continuing with the cramps and the heavy flow, I started to feel very sorry for myself. I didn't want to tell anyone what had happened this time. When the words came tumbling out of my mouth, they came with tears pricking my eyes. As I've said a few times, I'm not an emotional person but right now I felt broken, disheartened and I was starting to lose optimism, which is something I'd carried well throughout our journey.

And then there was Stage 4: depression. Or at least a depressive mood. I just needed a hug. The type where I could feel all warm, snuggly and safe. The type that only the hubby could give me. I never ask for hugs so when I do, he knows I really need one. So, there he was, just coming home from work and I was having a complete wobbler with myself so he wrapped his arms so tightly around me that I could just cry it out. I hoped that this cry would lift the cloud that had been consuming me for the last few days.

Breaking away from the hug, I immediately felt relief and started to feel that the world might not actually hate me. I was, however, still in two minds as to whether I should phone in sick for work. I was still in a lot of pain but I didn't want to phone and tell them why I was off sick. It's not like I could say I had a miscarriage. People know what that is. People don't understand what a chemical pregnancy is.

I popped in to see my friend later, who I didn't want to tell what was happening, as I knew his anxiety was bad and didn't want to add to it. I remembered that when my anxiety was bad, hearing about someone else's bad time took my mind off my own shit. That said, when I started explaining to him what had happened, it was harder to get the words out than I thought. I just remember saying after "Don't hug me, for god's sake don't hug me". I could feel the tears stinging my eyes again.

Walking back home after chatting it out, I decided that I would chance going into work and, if I got too bad, I'd just have to ask for relief. After all, it wasn't as if staying at home moping around was going to help me was it?!

Sitting at work the next day, knitting baby hats for other people, I started to delve into Stage 5: acceptance. I began to accept that this month simply wasn't our turn. Our turn would come and, as the Fairy Godmother says in Cinderella, "Even miracles take a little time".

The Wrong Diagnosis

When you go to the doctor's for thrush and come out with a test for chlamydia and a diagnosis you didn't even know you had.

Itch, itch go away and don't come back another day. Fuck right off and stay away! Thrush: the itch that keeps on giving. Vag as red raw as it can possibly get and don't dare mention cottage cheese to me again!

I sat, patiently waiting for my name to flash up on the screen. Ping. Thank God for that. I was seeing a nice doctor too. Knocking on the door with no answer, the doc appeared behind me and said "sorry, I was just getting your jab". Oh god, what injection did I need now?

The doc looked at me and asked how she could help. I began to explain that I'd got yet another thrush flare up, to the point that if I itched anymore, I was scared I wasn't going to have a fadge left! Obviously I didn't say the word *fadge* to the doctor. I was all prim and proper. But, because my floof had already gobbled one of those thrush killing tablets, the doc said that she wouldn't be able to do anything. If it happened again, I had to book in with the practice nurse when it was bad. I now have a lot more respect for practice nurses because I would not like to be staring at a thrushy fandango. F**k that shit.

So basically, you're telling me there was nothing you can do to stop it coming back?! "No, not really. Although you can do this test for me." She handed me a brown cardboard box. She then proceeded to ask me if I wanted my flu jab. Hang on one second, why the hell would I want that? And, since when am I entitled to it? Did having recurring thrush now give you the eligibility for the free flu jab?! "You have Idiopathic Intracranial Hypertension. That's why you can have it". Since when did I have that? And, more to the point, what the hell is it?

After the doc explained what it was, I had to ask whether I'd been given the wrong diagnosis as I'd been diagnosed with chronic migraines, not that long worded thing?! Turns out that, apparently I should've had some medical procedure before I left hospital back in 2015, but because it had been New Year's Day, I'd just been forgotten about by the sounds of it. I must say, Scunthorpe Hospital will be a place I will never forget,nor will I go back there, ever.

I left the doctor's surgery carrying my little cardboard box and a prescription for something or other feeling really puzzled. How the hell had the consultants forgotten to tell me that I had some long ass named disease? Disorder? Whatever the f**k it was. Oh how I wish I hadn't sat in the pharmacy and Googled it. Because, according to Google, my head would explode any day now. Clinging on tightly to my cardboard box, I contemplated sending numerous snotty emails demanding to be seen and consulted with but where would that get me? Nowhere, that's where.

Scrambling to collect everything from the pharmacist, I made it home in one piece and threw my keys and bag on the table. I began to open the cardboard box, thinking it must be a new test as I've had thrush before but never had to do a test for it. Was she f**king kidding me?! My doctor had only gone and sent me home with a test for Chlamydia. Now the questions about whether I was sexually active all made sense! I wasn't (and still aren't) some slapper that goes around sleeping with every willy I saw. I'm a one willy type of woman now. And that member belonged to the hubby!

The worst part of it all is that I'd carried that box through the busy doctor's surgery and the pharmacy. God knew what people must've thought. How embarrassing! Thank God I can laugh about it now. And thank God it was just a case of thrush. It still didn't excuse the doctor's for giving me a wrong diagnosis though. I wasn't sure what I was going to do with that one.

WHAT IF?

What if another Christmas rolled by and I still wasn't pregnant? Or what if we just enjoyed Christmas for what it was?

What if my body failed me again? Or what if it didn't?

What if I wasn't meant to be a mother? Or what if I was?

What if IVF failed for us? Or what if it didn't and it was our only chance at being successful?

What if that test I took 20 minutes ago, the one I threw in the bin, had turned positive? Or what if it was still a negative?

What if the test was negative again? Or what if it was positive this time?

What if my family thought I was a failure? Or what if they didn't, and they were proud of you for what you went through?

What if I was pregnant? Or what if it was just a late period and I got my hopes up?

What if the jealousy of yet another pregnancy announcement made me angry instead of joyous? What if that person was also struggling with infertility? Did they ever feel like this?

What if I carry the stamp of infertility for the rest of my life? Or what if I don't let infertility rule my existence.

What if the cramps I felt weren't period cramps, and they were implantation cramps, and I took painkillers, could I harm what could've been? Or what if it was simply period pain and there was no implantation?

What if I could never give my husband the child that he longed for to call him "daddy"? Or what if my husband supports and loves me no matter what happens?

What if I fell pregnant and we lost it? What if that pregnancy turned into a healthy little baby?

What if I wasn't strong enough? Or what if you were stronger than you thought?

What if I felt like giving up? Don't. Keep going because what if there really was light at the end of the tunnel?

What if I felt that I wasn't enough? What if you were enough? Keep going.

What if I stopped being so negative and started being positive? Would that help?

What if I stopped stressing about things I couldn't control?

What if there really was a rainbow after every storm? Go get yours because you deserve it!

What if, what if, what if...

Toxic

Have you ever realised that you can actually eliminate the toxicity from your life? And eliminate it for good?

Having toxic things in your life when you're struggling to conceive is a big no, no. I had found this out the hard way. And we're not just talking toxic people here, we're talking about food, drink, certain chemicals, all sorts - but not the liquorice ones.

There comes a time in your conception journey when it almost becomes obsessive; when you start to think that almost everything is bad for you, including people around you too. It also opens your eyes more. Well, it definitely did mine.

I realised at the beginning of our journey that there was a certain weed amongst my flowerbed, so to speak, but that weed was taking every bit of my sunshine on a daily basis, draining me constantly of everything I had: my self esteem, my personality, my being; and I began to diminish and wilt away. I was starting to become a weed myself.

I was finding myself eating away at someone close to me all because I was fighting for air. I realised that no amount of weed killer was going to eliminate this weed and it was starting to spread quicker than I could keep on top of it. The stress was starting to show: physically, mentally and emotionally. That was it. The weed needed to be plucked from the root so that it couldn't do anymore damage. The stress of trying to conceive was enough. I didn't have time to mess about with this as well.

A swift pluck and it was gone, albeit not without a fight. That fight nearly cost me dearly but to be weed-free was a breath of fresh air. That was until the weed came fighting back as a nettle, with an almighty sting, trying to hurt everyone that crossed its path, growing bigger in strength, and trying to take anything I had left away.

But I was not going to let the sting of this one nettle ruin me so, with every ounce of being I had left, I fought back. This nettle was not going to ruin my life and take away everything I had worked so hard for. I was going to eradicate this nettle no matter what it took. Even if it took months! This narcissistic nettle was not in control anymore. I was! No amount of their sting was going to kill my relationship. No amount of their poison was going to make me lose my job. I was on top of this!

The only thing I hadn't anticipated was the sting that the nettle was already leaving on others around me, making me question more of the situations in my life. I certainly didn't think one nettle could do this much damage but it was relentless and the damage in some cases was already done.

The nettle gradually gave up and died off come winter time, giving me time to flourish and fix relationships that were harmed during its being and I slowly began to relish life again. I was now able to start concentrating on trying to conceive again. I was ready. I was finally starting to feel more relaxed.

Someone once asked if I could ever forgive the weed for what they had done and the simple answer was no. I can't and nor will I ever forgive them for what they did to me. Even their apology is insufficient and insignificant because, quite frankly, they are so self-consumed they wouldn't have a clue what they were apologising for. They would just be saying words for the sake of it. Those words would certainly have no meaning coming from them.

2 years later and getting rid of that level of toxicity was the best decision of my life. It was an easy decision to make. It was like when I realised how milk made me feel ill and vomit, I wasn't going to go back and keep drinking the milk and making myself ill was I? That would simply be quite foolish don't you think?

Moral of the story

Some people are like flowers: they can inspire you. Others are like weeds: they can drain you.

Pick wisely.

Please excuse my infertility

Yes, you read that right. Never mind "Please excuse the elephant in the room!" Why? Because I am that elephant: me and my infertility. There was no use tip toeing around it anymore as it was here to stay. But seriously, some people needed to keep their advice to themselves. I was quite sick of having to hold my tongue to some of the stupid things people were coming out with.

Things not to say to someone who's dealing with infertility issues...

1. The old favourite: "*Just relax*". Bitch please. If I relax anymore, I may as well sleep until eternity.
2. "*Why don't you just adopt?*" Like it's that bloody simple! It's not like going to a zoo and picking out your favourite animal and going, "I'll pick and adopt you!"
3. *"Try IVF, I've heard it works well."* Said the most fertile person I know who's popped 3 kids out and who's never visited the clinic in their life.
4. "*My friend did this...* " Do I really look like I give a monkey's uncle what your friend did? Everyone's different.
5. *"Have you tried X, Y, Z...?"* Tried all 3 thanks and oh look still no baby.
6. *"2020 will be your year."* That's what you said about 2019 and look what happened then.

7. My favourite: *"Have you thought about cheating on your husband to have a baby?"* I don't think I even need to give you the answer to that one.
8. *"Just get more fur babies."* I love my dog but he's a one in a million.
9. *"Did you hear such and such is having a baby?"* Yes, I heard. Yes, I acknowledged. And yes, I'm happy for them. Now leave it the f**k alone.
10. *"Why don't you just stop trying? It worked for my friend."* Okay, so did your friend have to text their sperm donor every time she felt an egg burst from her ovary? Did your friend have to have every test under the sun to make sure they were actually ovulating? Did your friend actually have issues with both partners and not just that they'd tried once and it didn't happen?
11. My ultimate favourite: *"A chemical isn't a miscarriage; it was barely even there."* For me it was there enough for that stick to give me a second line, if only for a few days. Never tell a woman that it doesn't count because to them it's everything.

As much as you may think you're helping to give your advice, please be advised that everyone is different and everyone on their trying-to-conceive journey has different situations, so what worked for your fertile friend Freda isn't necessarily going to work for your infertile friend Irene. Before the words, "Have you tried...?" fall out of your mouth, stop! Retract and say "Isn't it nice weather we're having!" Or even better, "What can I do to support and help you on your journey?" These two little phrases mean the world to anyone going through the difficult conception journey so use them and heed some decent advice coming from someone who knows.

Blink. Just like that it was over

This was the raw truth. This is not going to be a happily ever after story right now. This was not our Christmas miracle like we expected. This was not some TV soap nor was it a fairytale. This was real life, my real life.

Let me take you back to November, where we knew it was an epic failure, where I fucked it up with the pee sticks and so I wrote it off and looked forward to our December cycle. We had our hopes very high, hoping for a Christmas miracle to top a shitty 2019. This would have made our year. But, like I said at the beginning, this isn't a fairytale and we didn't have our happy ending. What happened broke me. It broke my dreams and my Christmas spirit. Life is sometimes so cruel and there's literally nothing we can do about it...

December 4th: CD 14 and boom, I got a super positive on the smiley face detector pee sticks. Ovulation was imminent. It came at a great time as the hubby and I were going on our short vacation. This was something which we both needed, after holding off on holidays that year to make babies.

We had texted the donor to see if they were free, and luckily, they were available to help us out so insemination was done and now we waited. We enjoyed our time together over the weekend away, visiting London, Edinburgh and Glasgow. Even sleeping overnight on the Caledonian sleeper train, which was an experience in itself, and not a very comfortable one. Christmas markets galore and weird and wonderful museums - one of which smelt like dirty nappies to the point it was making me gag, yack! The hubby also surprised me with a trip to the theatre to watch the Lion King, which was truly amazing and I got so emotional with all the singing - simply outstanding!

Weekend over and it was time to go home. Back to reality and back to work. Back to bloody work! We got back on the 9th which meant I would've been approximately 5 DPO. I couldn't help but get my hopes up as I'd had loads of symptoms and I'd been none stop weeing all weekend. I would literally pee and then within an hour I'd need to pee again. It was crazy! I was holding out on my addiction as I didn't want to pee on sticks too early like all the other times before. I promised myself I would wait until Thursday. By then I'd be 9 DPO. It was still too early but I was going to start my night shifts and so I wouldn't be able to use the first morning pee.

Thursday came and went with a big fat negative. I would have to wait until Monday now. And anyone in the two week wait will understand how hard that is. I resisted and Monday soon came around. The tiniest of pink lines popped up on the stick. I convinced myself it was an evaporation line but I still had that pang of hope for our Christmas miracle.

On Tuesday, there it was: the second line; so dark it was unmistakable. My only concern was that I had been spotting, on and off, for the last 3 days. I didn't know what to think. What do you do? Well, I know what I did; I expected the worst. As soon as I saw the red smear on the loo roll, all my optimism disappeared.

Onto Wednesday, and I was having short bursts of cramps and I was still spotting. There was still a blazing positive on a cheap test but it was showing negative on the expensive ones. I knew it wasn't an evaporation line as it was there straight away unlike the other evaps I'd had; they'd always shown when they're dry and I've had to look twice. Never trust a test after it's been sat there for 5 minutes, unless it's a blazing positive.

After doing surplus Googling, I decided to take some advice from a site to figure out where the bleeding was coming from. They said to use the tampon trick. Pop a tampon up your vag and, if you pull it out and there's blood on it, it's more than likely coming from your cervix. Not what I wanted. So, guess what happened? I popped the tampon up and it came out clear. So where was this blood coming from?

There was only one person that I thought could help me: a doctor. Although I didn't actually hold out much hope for them helping. Ringing my doctor's surgery, I requested a call back as, before Christmas, appointments are like gold dust. After an hour waiting, the doctor called me back. All I needed was for her to either reassure me or tell me what I already knew that I was having another chemical. I told her everything and her response was that I'd just have to wait it out and retest in a week. Apparently spotting during early pregnancy can be normal unless the bleeding gets heavier and clots appear.

Great so now it was basically a waiting game. And waiting a week would take me to Christmas Day. What a fabulous present that would be. Not! Let the tears commence. The optimism left my body and left me feeling like utter shite!

On Thursday, the bleeding began, heavier than just spotting and the cramps started again, along with the tears and the hope. This pregnancy was leaving me. How many more chemicals can one person take? I know that I didn't think I could take any more heartbreak. The last one was bad enough. But just before Christmas, when everything is family and family orientated, it was like salt being rubbed into the wounds. Having to pretend to be okay, with a smile slapped on my face so I didn't get a million and one questions. There's only so much one person can take before they break. I just wanted to keep my strength so I could get through the Christmas period and then start a new page in 2020.

Blink. Just like that it was over.

New Year, New Journey

IVF: got this. Nope, IVF: not got this. IVF: shit my pants just thinking about it.

Could you guess what we're doing next week? I bet you can't. Of course, you guessed right, we were starting IVF. Come the 9th of January our journey was changing. Although I knew it was coming to this, I don't think my mind quite did.

Since booking the first appointment, my anxiety just wouldn't fuck off. It was the kind of anxiety you literally can't reason with. You literally kick your own arse with. Nothing your brain is doing is making you feel any better, crying in the shower because something didn't go your way today is not a sane response. Yes, that was me. The girl who cried in the shower when shit went down and I couldn't cope. I don't cry on people. I never have and I never will. I sometimes think I'm probably a psychiatrist's dream with some of my deep-rooted issues but who doesn't have issues these days?!

So come the 9th of January we would be told whether or not we could go ahead with IVF. I didn't see why we wouldn't be able to as my BMI was finally under the 35 we needed for the clinic we were about to use. And trust me, these clinics are like rocking horse shit - hard to come by!

When I phoned the clinic and said my BMI was above the loved 30 (I was at 31.4) I waited for the discrimination to start, about how my weight was going to be an issue yet again but no, I was greeted with, "As long as it's under 35 we're happy to take you on." I nearly shrieked down the phone when the receptionist said those words to me.

How I've longed to be accepted and not told, "Fuck off fat bitch." Okay, so they might not say it in those exact words but they may as well do because that's how I come away feeling. I mean, what do they expect me to do, have gastric surgery or something? Oh yeah, I already did that to please the Gods, aka the gynae squad! Even after having the gastric band fitted, and losing a shit tonne of weight, I was still turned away by the NHS; I'm still not good enough in their eyes. I was so lucky that the Darlington Clinic would see us and are willing to take a chance on us.

I had no idea what to expect when we got there. This was probably why my anxiety was sky high. Yet again it was something out of my control and I didn't like it. The only thing I knew was that this was our only way forward, the only way we were going to be able to make a baby. So I had to have hope because without hope, what's left?

What I did know is that I had a date with Wanda on Thursday. Good old Wanda, always ready to have a good poke around your lady parts, letting you know that yep, you're still a woman and everything's in its rightful place. I'd also been made aware that I would have to have more bloods taken. I really want to say that I hate needles here, but considering IVF will make me overcome my fear, because I'll be stabbing myself every day for a while, I'm sure one little blood test couldn't hurt me could it?! I'd just make sure I had the best nurse on the team doing it. There's always that one nurse who deals with the 'awkward' patients aka me. Me and my tiny useless veins. The veins that see a needle and go "Fuck this, I'll collapse so I can't be stabbed." I don't want another in, out, in, out shake it all about drama, like I had in the doctor's surgery the other week or they'd be passing me the sick bucket.

So, here's the serious part: after our last chemical pregnancy, and the doctors literally refusing to do jack shit for me, apart from telling me to go to a clinic, or that the donor we're using might not have been compatible with me, that was my final straw. It's what made me make the call.

I do have to say this though, even though we're not using our original donor on our new journey, he will forever be in our hearts for what he has done for us. He helped us when nobody else would. His family supported not only his decision to help us, but supported us through the entire process and for that we are eternally grateful. Words just can't express our gratitude for them. They are the type of human beings I thought had all but been eradicated from this time. True friends.

Making dreams a reality

The night before our first ever appointment at our new clinic, The London Women's Clinic in Darlington, after just finishing our tea, I said to the hubby "we need a list." Everyone who I had spoken to that had been through IVF said we should go with a list of questions, written down, because, as the time comes, your mind will go blank.

So, upon this advice, we started our list. First came the simple questions like *how long does the process take?* And *does the hubby need to be there for every appointment due to work commitments?* Then came the more complex questions such as: *will we get to pick the donor, or is it done for us?* And, *when the eggs are removed, am I put under general anaesthetic, or just sedated?* (this bit I was literally shitting my pants about). We ended up with a list of about 6 different questions that we'd both put together.

Going to bed that night was hard. I was so excited and nervous all in one go and my stomach doesn't handle all that excitement. It was one of those situations where you daren't fart; I'll leave it at that.

Waking up at 5am, I felt like it was Christmas when I was a child. I had a belly full of butterflies and was anticipating what would happen during the day. Placing my head back on the pillow, I drifted off again, only to wake, what felt like moments later, to cock-a-doodle-doo. I love that alarm tone. It makes me jump out of bed every time because it's the most annoying sound ever!

I'd already had a shower the night before but, knowing I had a date with Wanda, I thought I'd best have a freshen up again. I didn't want to give the poor doctor a nose full. Shower done and a shit tonne of talcum powder coating my froo froo, I finally felt clean enough to get dressed. But what to wear? I already had my socks and pants picked out, as underwear is all the same, but what top should I wear? Should you go smart or smart casual? Why didn't I pick my clothes out the night before?! Picking out my new jeans and a stripy top, I felt fabulous. I also had to remember that I would be getting weighed so didn't want to wear heavy clothing and for them to tell me it was a no go.

We stressed about every little thing before we left the house. *Did we have the letters from the GP? Did we have our list of questions? Our IDs? Our payment?* The list was endless but we were finally on our way, not before I managed to drop everything at the front door. Chasing my smear test results around the front garden was not what I needed! Finally, I was sat in the car ready to go.

After an hour and a bit of driving, we arrived early. The hubby's always early for everything but me, on the other hand, will be the type of person that is late to their own funeral. Walking into the hospital, I felt my stomach go yet again so headed straight for the loo. Unfortunately, there was someone else in there and I was just too scared to fart and for them to laugh. I'd just die with embarrassment and I didn't need that today.

Leaving the loo and trying not to think about it, we headed for the sign that said London Women's Clinic on it. Opening the big double hospital doors, we were greeted by a lovely smiley receptionist who completely put us at ease with her calm and gentle manner. We were told to take a seat and someone would be with us shortly. She also said there was a drinks machine and toilet around the corner. And so the hubby disappeared and came back with a hot chocolate and a decaf coffee for me.

All I could think about was the toilet. Relief. Opening the toilet door, I finally felt comfortable enough to take in my surroundings. The wall in front of me caught my eye as it was covered in baby pictures and I mean covered! I would say it kind of ruined the 80's theme they had going on but then I couldn't really as the babies were just so damn cute! We later found out that that was only a small portion of the babies that had been created there. So much hope and optimism pictured on that one wall.

After sitting for a little while, we were called through to meet our nurse. Yes, we had our very own nurse and she too was so friendly. So friendly indeed that all my worries were swept away when we started talking.

My height and weight were checked and not a word said about the fact my BMI was slightly on the high side. I'd never felt so relieved. I was even given good news to the fact that I was now 5'5, and not my previous 5'4, which meant that the chiropractor I'd been seeing had actually worked. My spine was starting to straighten and boy would I appreciate that extra inch - like any girl would!

After all my checks and our little chat, I was told that I'd be getting to meet Wanda. The hubby had asked me before we had entered the clinic if he could watch as he was intrigued as to what happens and also wanted to see my insides! Entering the Wanda room, I was shocked to see no bed. There was only a chair. Until then I'd only ever had the ultrasound laid down so sitting up was a new experience but, in all honesty, it was much better sitting or rather slouching to have Wanda check me out.

The nurse left the room and as we sat waiting for her to come back, in walked this man. Well, I looked at the hubby and the hubby looked at me and we both thought the same thing, "Who the hell is this?!" Turns out it was our consultant. Me, personally, I think that that was done a bit backwards. I would've generally liked to shake my consultants' hand first before he got to see my vajayjay but it's just one of those things isn't it. Scan completed and I was told I have a healthy uterus and no visible cysts on my ovaries. Had I been misdiagnosed yet again? Who knows. I'm past fighting with doctors and their shit diagnoses.

The consultant then left the room and I was handed some tissue to discover just how much KY jelly was used. I bloody hate that stuff! After I was all clean again, we left the room and headed back to the waiting room for more form filling and another cheeky hot chocolate; don't mind if I do!

We were then called into the consultant's room, who finally introduced himself, but once again he was so lovely that I couldn't bring myself to say anything. He explained in depth the procedures he could offer us, including IUI and IVF. We chose IVF as, technically, we had already been doing something similar to IUI at home and it hadn't really worked as we'd hoped. Also, the chances of IUI being successful were rather low compared to the 50-60% success rate of IVF.

We sat and listened and at the end he asked if we had any questions. Some of the questions we had written down he had already covered so we skimmed past them. But we asked the main questions, like *how long it would take?* etc and was shocked to find out that from start to finish it would take approximately 4 weeks. I thought it was going to be months not weeks so I was rather relieved shall we say.

We were told we would have to have counselling before we could go ahead and that appointment was booked for us right there and then for the 29th January at 1pm. We were also told to check out the sperm donor database to pick out our sperm. This was much harder than it sounded I'll tell you!

Walking away from the appointment, my nerves had disappeared and the excitement was oozing out of both the hubby and I. He said giddily to me "Oh my god, we're going to have a baby!" I do think he was a bit more excited than me because, as much as I was excited, I still had the "What if it doesn't work" looming in the back of my mind. But right then, right at that moment, that's where it stayed and I replied to him, "yes, yes we are, finally our dream can become a reality!"

The minefield of donor sperm

3 weeks goes so slowly when you're patiently waiting for an appointment. Well, at least trying to be patient. That definitely wasn't one of my strong points.

A week into our 3 week wait, we started to search for our new sperm donor. This was something that we thought would be easy but, of course, it was anything but. My hubby has dark hair, brown eyes, and olive coloured skin, exactly like me so we knew that the donor had to somewhat try and match this.

We had decided to go for a donor with a Mediterranean look as countless times when we've been to the U.S, we've had people coming up to us and trying to have a conversation in Spanish. Then when we say we're English, they are shocked. So after talking about it for what seemed like a lifetime, we thought it was a no brainer because the only Caucasian man on the donor site had blue eyes and red hair. That was definitely a no go for us. Not because we're being picky, but we don't want to have to answer a million and one questions. Or for people to assume that I had an affair. You all know how it goes. People have weird perceptions of things that they know nothing about and so they just assume the worst. It's human nature. And it's called gossip! We wanted to be open, and honest to any child of ours about where they came from. We are not ashamed of how, or why we were having to go through IVF. It is what it is. What we don't want is for our child to have to answer awkward questions when, with simple donor elimination, that is all avoidable.

Picking our donor was nothing like what you see in every over the top American movie. You don't get to go into a beautiful office, sit on a nice comfy sofa and flip through a folder with a shit tonne of donor pictures in it so you can at least see some resemblance. All you get, in most cases, is a short description and the basic knowledge of eye colour, hair colour, race etc. The people conducting these donor interviews do a fabulous job but when you're sat there, staring at a computer screen, trying to picture your future child, it's not easy I'll tell you. It's not like when you first meet the love of your life and you can see every inch of them and you start to imagine what your children will look like. We didn't get that. We got to know that they liked football or worked as a computer tech or have a good sense of humour; it's just not the same but it's all we had. We found our perfect match on week 2 of the search but we were told by our clinic that we couldn't order it until we had been to see the counsellor. And so the wait was on.

The next day I decided to have another look at our chosen donor only to find that it was no longer available to UK clinics. This was where our nightmare started.

Most of the donors on the London sperm bank site were either Chinese or Indian which wasn't something we were looking for. We had about a handful of choices to go from so it was absolutely gutting that we had lost our pick and we still had another 2 weeks to wait.

I emailed the company to ask why it wasn't available to the UK and found out that donors are only allowed to donate to 10 families within the UK. Once the tenth family has bought the sperm, then it's taken off sale. I was annoyed to say the least. We were losing out on what we wanted all because the clinic didn't have the appointment space for the counsellor.

3 more days passed and 3 more potential donors disappeared. We were left with 2 and still had another week to wait. I decided then not to look on the site until the day before our appointment as each time I looked, it pissed me off a little bit more.

The time to our appointment seemed to pass so slowly, to the point I thought time had stood still. Eventually we were there. Only one more sleep to go so I logged back onto the site to find once again we were left with slim pickings. One donor had the words 'Contact clinic' with them but they seemed like a perfect match so I knew I had to enquire. Although now part of me wishes I never had as, once again, only disappointment came our way. This donor only wanted his sperm to go to a homosexual couple or a single woman and it specifically said IUI only. So that was it, another one binned off. And then there were 2.

2 donors; 2 totally different backgrounds. It was now or never for us. We had to pick. Each donor had something within their genes that made us question using them but we had to simply use a process of elimination to see through it. Eventually there was one! Our donor was picked and we were feeling much more relaxed about walking into our appointment. Though we still had to wait 24hours before we could pay for it and secure it. That time flew by and, before we knew it, our 07:30am

alarm was buzzing away. Just one more snooze should do it.

The appointment

Some mornings I just can't get up, especially if I've been on an early shift at work I'm literally exhausted. This morning was just one of them. The type where you fall out of bed, crawl to the toilet, and then after a quick face wash with cold water, you don't resemble a sloth anymore.

Face washed, makeup caked on, and hair somewhat brushed back, it was breakfast time. But my stomach just wasn't in the mood for breakfast. I had that nervous, rumbling tummy feeling, the one where everyone can hear it growl. I brushed it off thinking it would be okay but boy was I wrong. The 2 hour drive to the hubby's parents' house seemed to pass in a sweaty brow, arse nipping blur. But I made it. Hallelujah! Praise the toilet! When IBS strikes, it strikes with a vengeance and usually when you don't want it to!

After completing a few jobs at the in-laws', it was time for us to get to our appointment and luckily my stomach had decided to behave itself for the journey. That was until we got to the clinic. After more form filing and a quick chat with the friendly receptionist, we were called into the dinky little room by the counsellor. This session I had been dreading as we thought it was some sort of a test but it actually turned out to be anything but.

Janet was lovely and answered all of our questions and gave us loads more information, that even we weren't aware was out there, even after the amount of research we'd done. Then we got talking about our donor and why we'd picked them etc. We were then asked if we'd already bought the sperm but we explained to her that we were told we had to wait until after this meeting. I don't know who was more shocked: her or us as it was a load of crap. So apparently, all the perfect matches we could've used had gone because we were fed some misinformation. That being said, the donor we had now picked sounded just as perfect as the rest.

As soon as we left Janet's office, I was straight onto the London sperm bank purchasing our donor as I wasn't willing to wait any longer! We weren't sat down for long before we were called in to see the nurse for my blood tests, something I'd been dreading. I usually only have one nurse that takes my bloods because of my shitty little veins so I wasn't sure how I was going to get on.

I ended up sending the hubby to wait in reception as my anxiety hit the roof and I just couldn't cope with him being there or seeing me like that. The poor nurse had to give me a good 5 minutes to pump my vein up and then both the vein and I were ready. Sharp scratch and it was over.

Now to pee in the cup. Why is it when you have to pee you get a shy bladder? It just seems to shrivel up and laugh at you when it does it. 3 cups of water later and my bladder feeling like it's fit to burst, I headed to the bathroom to find it was a dribble. Seriously, just pee goddamn it. With a little bit of gentle persuasion, and a whole lot of forcing, and water dripping from the tap, the sample pot was adequately filled. I just had to make sure there were no leaks and I could hand it over to the nurse with ease.

Nothing's ever simple for me though. No sooner as I had departed the toilet, we were called into the consultants room with a pocket full of pee and all I could think was "Oh god please don't explode!" It didn't help that I kept having to touch the bottle to make sure it was still there and that it hadn't leaked all over the floor. Honestly, my anxiety was through the roof that day.

We sat discussing different injections and medications with the consultant and I felt like he was talking in a foreign language. He might as well have with all the stuff we had to remember. Luckily our nurse was on hand to give us a step by step guide and to also take my pee away for testing. It was also happening a lot sooner than I expected too. Dates, medication and my period all discussed within a small appointment and we finally had our plan in place. The plan that would hopefully change our lives forever.

I bounced out of that room with a big spring in my step. Nothing could wipe that smile off my face. That was until we were slapped with the bill which was a lot higher than expected - and I mean a lot! Their website proclaimed that 3 rounds of IVF was £6600, which we thought was perfect. We knew that the sperm would cost us £1050 extra. But what we didn't expect was the fees for the medication. Even if you have an NHS prepayment card, it doesn't mean shit when it comes to IVF meds. So that would come to a grand total of £850. We then had blood tests to pay for, and anaesthesia to pay for, and the list goes on.

All in all, it came in at just under £10,000 for 3 goes. But, here's another one for you, you can only use this deal on fresh cycles. If you wanted a frozen transfer, it would be an extra £1200. And the deal is only valid for one year. So you couldn't technically have 2 babies out of it. But we went with it, as it's not guaranteed to work the first time so at least now we had a back up. Although that's still not the point. The fact that they advertise one price and don't tell you the real price until everything's set in stone is very annoying. I know it's not the clinic's fault; it's the company who run it that way but I daren't complain until after it's over - just in case they fuck it up for us. I'm not saying that they would do that but my mind was in overdrive yet again. I was constantly overthinking everything.

After having the price thrown at us, my bouncy energy depleted and left me feeling like absolute shit: annoyed and emotional. The fact that we now had to find an extra £2000 from somewhere was stressful. It's at times like these when I wish money trees were real!

Although, just before closing the door behind me, I couldn't help but smile to myself, knowing that the next time we would walk through them we would be at the start of our journey into IVF. It would be real and not just talked about. So, even after walking out of there feeling slightly disappointed, my mood was once again lifted with the prospect of what was to come.

Hormotional

My new favourite word: hormotional. I'm not even on the hard core IVF drugs yet, just some tablets so they can control my periods. The same tablets they give you if you don't want your period on holiday. The same tablets that, up until now, I didn't know existed. If the side effects weren't so bad on me, I would definitely use them again because who wants good old Aunt Flo to show up, full throttle whilst you're swanning around on the beach in that brand new white bikini? Yep me neither.

A few days into the packet of Norethisterone and I already noticed a change in myself. I constantly felt angry and not just a little bit either; it was like I could literally blow my top at any second and that's something that's not in my temperament, unless someone's pissed me off and keeps poking the bear, then they're asking for trouble. No, *bear* is not a euphemism. But right there and then I wasn't getting poked or anything. I just felt like I wasn't in control of my own body, like that little subdued devil inside me had started to surface and they weren't going to go away until they'd had their say. It was very much like a toddler wanting something they know they can't have. That type of irrational behaviour that no one wants to deal with. That being said, I seemed to control it pretty good. Until I didn't.

Like the day me and the hubby had decided to take some time out to go watch a movie at the cinemas, and some silly girl hadn't looked as she pulled out of the junction. No sorry, no fuck all from her, that literally turned me into a raging loon. I was shouting and pointing; it wasn't like she could hear me anyway. The poor hubby on the other hand just looked at me, with that look of sheer astonishment in his face, and then asked me if I felt better after that. What a stupid question. Of course I didn't. I was in 'that' mood. That one you just can't shift. It's like a dark cloud descends and then everything goes black. I knew I had to snap out of it but, as I'd never felt like this, I didn't know how.

After having a lovely afternoon, we trundled home, where a new feeling hit, of complete sadness. All I wanted to do was cry and cry and cry. And I knew that if I started, I may not be able to stop. Slightly dramatic I know but that's how everything felt - like I'd just stepped into a soap and I was aiming for world's best actress title. Except I wasn't acting, I was living it.

A few days later, and a few night shifts later, I rang the hubby first thing in the morning, as I always do, one to keep me awake until I got home, and two, to make sure he had actually gotten out of bed and was on route to work. This morning in particular I was feeling it from the minute I'd left work, my anxiety had crept high. I was hitting every milestone where I knew I was heading for trouble. I just about managed to keep my head above water for the drive home. I can vaguely remember the phone call with the hubby. The phone call where I decided that I hated him for no apparent reason but then cried because I didn't really hate him. I felt like I'd totally lost control. All he had said is that he couldn't wait until I was off these tablets, and he had his old Kelly back. But those words were like a red rag to my raging bull and I had to hang up the phone. I then had to stop and text minutes later apologising for my awful behaviour.

I managed to get home and thought a good day's sleep was all I needed. How wrong I was. That mood just wouldn't shift. It got so bad at one point that I remember thinking "if he doesn't turn down the brightness on his phone screen, I'm going to launch it out of the window". It was at that point that I took myself out of the room. I felt like I was losing control of myself. I knew I only had two more days left of those tablets and it couldn't come quick enough as I couldn't put up with myself any longer. The poor hubby was running out of egg shells to not even tread on anymore - he was running on the fuckers!

2 days passed and the last tablet swallowed, all I had to do now was wait for good old Mr Blobby to show up. The clinic had said that it would take between 3-5 days for it to show after stopping the last tablet. I wasn't holding my breath as my body has a mind of its own, one where it defies all rules. Although on this occasion, it had behaved itself and turned up right on schedule which meant that, now the doctors were in control of my menstrual cycle, we could go onto phase 2. The wait was on and I was definitely in a much better mood all round - well, at least to the point where I wanted to kill the hubby a little less.

1 down, 15 more to go

After my period showed up right on schedule, we knew we were all systems go. With my first baseline scan booked, we were finally there: finally starting our new journey to becoming parents. And, let me tell you, I was shitting my pants at the thought of it all. I had such an overwhelming sensation pulsating through my body. I almost felt like I was in fight or flight mode, not knowing what was going to happen to us in the next few weeks and not knowing if all the shit I was about to put my body through would even give us our happy ending. That being said, I still had hope. Hope that was oozing out of me with all its glowing positivity. The hope that I held onto with all of my might.

During the days leading up to my baseline scan, I started to feel unwell. Day after day I just told myself it was a cold until the day I finally gave in and realised I couldn't kid myself anymore. This was more than a cold. I felt like absolute shit. Every time I coughed, a strong pain stabbed me in my lung, leaving me in agony. Every time I swallowed, it was as if I was swallowing a thousand razor blades and my nose was like a constant tap with no chance of stopping. The tiredness didn't even just creep over me, it hit me in the face like a bag of bricks, making me crave my bed. The problem was that every time I laid down, I started to cough; and every time I coughed, I would tire myself out. It was a never ending merry-go-round - one I really wanted to get off.

I dragged my sorry arse to the doctors knowing I needed antibiotics. I also knew that my doctor's surgery is rather reluctant to give them out but I knew I had to try. After one hour sat patiently waiting, I was called in. After explaining my symptoms and a quick exam, I was told that I had a chest infection and sinusitis. However, in the next breath, I was told that antibiotics wouldn't help as I'd only been symptomatic for two weeks. I had to be blunt and tell her that we were starting IVF in 7 days and I needed to be fit and well so there was no way I was leaving without antibiotics. She eventually relented and gave me some but what I didn't realise was that she hadn't given me the normal ones I'd usually have - that actually work - she'd given me a brand I'd never heard of. I had a quick Google only to find that someone who is going through fertility treatments or pregnancy should not be given this type. I wouldn't have minded but I specifically told her that we were starting our fertility treatment in a week's time. All I could think was that it never rains, it bloody well pours. I couldn't help but feel emotional and helpless to it all. Could this one little cold scupper our chances of our first IVF round already?

After I'd had my emotional breakdown to myself on the sofa, I rang our clinic to ask them if it changed anything as I didn't need anymore stress. Luckily they called me back almost immediately to give me the good news that, as long as I wasn't taking the antibiotics by the time we came to transfer, all was well and good. There was the light at the end of the tunnel I needed - for then anyway. It was enough to make me drag my sorry arse to bed, where I stayed for almost a week as my body tried to fight off the bug.

I finally arose on the day of our baseline scan appointment. The scan I hadn't really been looking forward to; who wants Wanda poking around when you're on your period? Definitely not me! I couldn't think of anything worse. The only thing that should be shoved up there at that time of the month is a tampon or Mooncup. No Wanda's or penises, thank you very much!

Before we went to the clinic, we decided to set off earlier so we could spend a bit of time at the beach. We were hoping the sea air would make us feel better because, by then, the poor hubby was also suffering the wrath of my cold/flu/chest infection. Parking up and walking around, we found a huge arcade filled with games with cheap pound shop toys in them. The ones where if you've got kids with you, you end up spending at least £10 to get a £1 toy. But at least it's fun for them and that's all that matters, right?! After spending said £10 and walking away with two £1 toys, I felt like it was time to go. I'd got what I went in for - another Disney keyring. The random Monopoly toy was a bonus!

When we got back to the car, we both looked at each other and I said "Next time we come here, I could have a baby in my belly or we could have one in a pram". This scan meant so much to us as it was the beginning of our new journey and hopefully an end to all the heartache and sorrow that we'd been through the last few years.

The scan was quick, simple and almost pain free so I was rather relieved. We even got to keep the scan pictures, even if it was only of my empty insides. We knew that hopefully next time we'd be looking at a scan picture that would contain our child.

We were given the green light to start the injections that same night to kick start my ovaries into producing eggs. That was the part I was least looking forward to, having to psych myself up to stab myself each night but, in all honesty, it wasn't half as bad as what I'd thought it would be. The needle slid through my skin like a knife to butter and just like that it was done. 1 down, 15 more to go.

How do you like your eggs in the morning?

4 days into the nightly injection routine, the routine changed as I had to add in a new one called Fyremadel. This little beggar I hadn't been looking forward to as it was meant to be an 'ouchy' one. Nurse Jackie had already warned me about it and so had a few girls I know that have been through IVF themselves.

One hour it took me to psych myself up to stab myself with that. The other injection, that contained my Menopur, was a nice simple painless injectable - nothing like Fyremadel. I sat there at the dining room table, with the needle hovering an inch away from my skin, praying that it didn't hurt too much. Stab. Oh that doesn't feel too… ouch, ouch, ouch, yes it did feel stingy. It was like the time when I was a child and a wasp landed on my middle finger, stung me and flew off. That initial ouch is exactly what that felt like. Then came the itch, the sting, and the swell - in that order. It may have only lasted for an hour but by heck that hour seemed to last forever.

The next nightly injection was exactly the same but I just powered on through it, with a feeling of elation as I'm not sure what the Menopur contained. All I know is that I felt like I was queen of the world and I was on cloud nine and nothing was going to ruin my mood. Nothing. I hadn't felt this good in years. My depressed mood had lifted; my daily anxieties were gone. I wanted to stay on this drug forever. I would take the bad side effects just to keep the good ones. Although I say they were "bad side effects" they weren't actually too bad. Except the constant bloating and the pain in my ovaries which weirdly spread to my bum hole so I constantly felt I needed a poo!

The only upside to the bad side effects was that I could clear the room with one fart. They were almost what I would call *epic*. I know that's gross but usually it's the hubby or the dog that fart me out of the room. Now even the poor dog was trying to bury his head in his bed; trying to escape the stench floating from one's butt hole! On the plus side, it meant that I got the TV remote control whilst he ran from my stench.

The Menopur effect.

The good side effects started almost immediately. I had the feeling of contentment flowing through my body, making me super chilled out, and super loved up. Both were feelings I'd not felt in such a long time. Next came the constant randiness. 3 days in and I was telling the hubby we had to go home and jump straight in the sack. And, oh my god, the orgasms. Wow! I'd never felt anything like it! I wish I could be on Menopur forever. I'd almost forgotten what a sex drive was. I think my fandango had somewhat shrivelled up and died a few years ago so I don't think the hubby knew what had hit him. Not that he complained anyway!

The only downside to feeling constantly horny, and being extremely fertile was the, what will forever be known as, fanny bogeys. Oh dear God, it was so embarrassing. At one point I ran to the loo thinking I'd peed my pants only to find the pesky fanny bogeys oozing out of me. My fandango had turned into my nose when I had a cold. Nightmare! And so not sexy at all!

The first few days on the Menopur passed in a tired, horny state and then I broke the barrier on Day 6 and I felt fabulous. But I was bloated. Day 6 was also our scan day to see how many follicles I was harbouring. I certainly wasn't disappointed with the number. A whopping 17! No wonder I was so bloated.

3 more days passed and we had what would hopefully be our last scan. I walked in happy and optimistic and walked out feeling sad and disappointed. We were told we were right on track for egg collection in 2 days,

which was fab news and just what we wanted to hear. And then we heard the *but*. That one word no one wants to hear as it's usually followed by something negative. Our doctor didn't disappoint. We were told that they could go ahead with egg collection as planned but, as I was at high risk of OHSS, (Ovarian Hyperstimulation Syndrome), we might have to put the transfer on hold to give my body a chance to rest.

We headed home after our good news/bad news situation and we were trying to stay positive but it wasn't happening. The negativity started to creep in and I felt once again like my body was failing me. All I kept saying was "We've waited so long. I can't wait any longer." Then the hubby would say "Look how long we've waited, what's 6 more weeks?!" 6 weeks in my head right there felt like an eternity. We still didn't know whether we would have to wait or not yet but the stress of it started to take over and I just wanted to scream. So I went to sleep instead.

Waking up somewhere between Darlington and York, I had decided that I had a craving for Sushi - not even pregnant yet and the cravings had already hit - so we detoured into York to allow me to satisfy said craving. We had to eat quickly as we also had to be home for 20:30 hrs because I needed to inject the trigger shot in time for egg collection 36 hours later.

We made it home just in time and I administered the shot. The wait was on, although it went pretty quickly, as it was soon the following night and we were on our way to the hotel. But not before a quick stop off to meet up with some of the hubby's friends. The only people who had really supported him throughout our entire IVF journey. The ones who had wished us both luck every time we had a procedure or we injected. I told the hubby that friends like those are hard to come by and I thanked them for being his rock in all of this. Me, I'm exceptionally lucky that I have a great support system. I don't know where I would be without my friends and family pushing me along.

Sitting in a rather packed pub talking about our next procedure and how it was done, and mentioning the words vagina and sperm quite a few times, was the highlight of my night. If people could've heard, I bet they thought we were a set of right raunchy buggers but I wasn't bothered. The word *vagina* gets thrown around in our house more times in a day than "hello"!

An hour or two passed in a blur and then it was time for bed but I knew I wouldn't be able to sleep. I was too excited, for one, and two, I was anxious as shit! I saw a few o'clock before I eventually gave in and got up at 06:20am in time for a shower to make myself feel a bit better. It also gave me time to watch some crap on TV so it would chill me out before we left for the short walk to the hospital.

Walking into the clinic, it was silent and empty. I even double checked the time to see if we were too early but no, we were right on time. We only sat for about 5 minutes before I was called through but I was taken aback as it wasn't our usual nurse Jackie. It was a different one. I didn't like that and it pushed my anxiety higher. But I coped, until the new nurse came in with a paper kidney dish containing 3 white little bullets, and a splodge of KY Jelly. Then she really wasn't my friend.

At the point of me being handed the suppositories, I told the hubby to get himself off and go get some breakfast from the hotel. No one wants to see my arse before eating their breakfast. Although the hubby offered to 'help', I swiftly declined and sent him on his way. Walking out of that toilet 5 minutes later was not a feeling I would like to have again, desperately trying to nip my butt cheeks together so I didn't fart out the bullets, whilst really trying hard not to look like I'd actually shit myself.

I needn't have sat down as, before I even had a chance to check my phone, I was escorted into the procedure room, where I was met by the wonderful nurse Jackie! Anxiety now at a steady 6, I laid down waiting for the anaesthetist to tell me he couldn't find a vein but instead I heard the words "sharp scratch." As the cold liquid hit my bloodstream, I started to feel sleepy and then black.

I woke up with the other nurse saying my name and trying to get me to drink as my blood pressure was a little on the low side. Water is my least favourite drink so I felt much better when she brought me some tea and biscuits. I drifted in and out of sleep before I was awoken and the hubby was there to collect me. Only I couldn't go yet as my bladder had decided to go shy, which meant I had to sit and wait in the waiting room and drink cold water until I went. It took me 30 minutes but I eventually went and, that was it, I had opened the floodgates.

We were told before we left that I was at a very high risk for developing OHSS and I was given a form to take home in case I ended up in hospital. Yes, apparently it can get that bad! We were also told that they wouldn't transfer if I had OHSS as a pregnancy could exacerbate the condition. In the next breath, we were told we had 18 eggs! I guessed 20 from the start so I had high hopes. We wouldn't know until the next day how many had actually fertilised but again I had egg-ceedingly high hopes for my little chicks and guessed 13.

It turns out my little chicks are over achievers and we had a whopping 14! Not all of them would make it to the 5-day old blastocyst stage. But how many survive? We wouldn't know that for a few days.

Officially PUPO

As of the 16/03/20 we were officially PUPO.

We headed to the clinic at 11:15am anxiously awaiting to be told whether or not we could transfer, due to my blood tests coming back high and the doctor telling us that, because they were that high, it would be very likely that I'd have OHSS - the syndrome no women wants while awaiting IVF! Luckily for us, I hadn't had any symptoms - aside from really bad bloating and some serious gas!

As we were walking towards the little changing rooms, I realised that within the next 10 mins we would either be so overwhelmed with happiness, or feeling like our dreams had been squashed. All adorned with my sexy hospital gown, I started to help the hubby with his. He was super excited that he was allowed in the treatment room with me. As it was a sterile room, we didn't think he would be allowed but, as long as he wore his gown and what will forever be known as shoe condoms, he was!

It was time to walk into the procedure room, and I was absolutely shitting myself. I was so nervous that I constantly felt like I needed to fart and I was not going to let that slip - the poor doctor's face would be in the direct line! The feeling of the fart disappeared as the nurse pressed hard on my stomach to assess my ovaries. I now had the urge to pee and, when you're laid there, legs in stirrups and you have a speculum up your floof, you can't even try to hold it in. I just had to grin and bear it whilst gripping the hell out of the hubby's hand!

The green go ahead light was given. The doctor went and implanted our little 4AA chick (yes, all blastocysts get graded, and ours were all hitting high grade marks). The hubby was mesmerised as, when the doctor placed it inside of me, he could see it on the screen. I was so glad he got to see it because all I could see was a lovely view of the nurse's bum. I did get to see it afterwards in the photos and it was so emotional. I didn't cry but I had a weird sensation in my stomach of such love for this little white blob!

Symptoms Galore

Key for IVF jargon:

DP - *days passed*

5DT - *5-day transfer*

PUPO - *pregnant until proven otherwise*

BFP - *big fat positive*

BFN - *big fat negative*

OTD - *official test day*

Transfer day: I felt nothing really, just normal but I was still bloated from the egg collection.

1DP 5DT: There was slight cramping and a pulling sensation behind my belly button. I do remember the nurse saying that the blastocyst should implant 24-48 hours after transfer so fingers crossed.

2DP 5DT: I was back to work tonight. Again, there was some slight cramping but luckily the bloating had somewhat gone down now so I could see my feet again.

3DP 5DT: I woke up feeling really dizzy, like the feeling after a heavy night on the gin. There was still some slight cramping and it now seemed to be sporadic, rather than just at night. I also had a weird craving for wholemeal toast - and I hate brown bread (fecking hormones)!

4DP 5DT.. I awoke to a really weird feeling in my stomach. It could have been the half packet of Liquorice Allsorts that I'd consumed the night before. I also had the worst case of the shits I've had in a while but, once it was done, I felt loads better. I still felt a little dizzy but that could've still all been side effects of the Progesterone tablets I was now on. I was cramping on and off but then it seemed to have died right off. Let's hope it was implantation. The craving for wholemeal toast was still with me and it took the nausea away.

5DP 5DT: I was only halfway through and I promised the hubby I would pee on a stick. I'd only ordered them the previous day so they weren't due for delivery until that afternoon. I pulled out one of my back up cheap tests and found myself staring at the test: front ways, backward, upside down and saw the faintest sniff of a line. But, as it was only a cheap test, I dismissed it.

When Amazon delivered my First Response, and I couldn't help myself, I peed on a stick. My hubby had been having a shit day so I decided to hopefully make it better... 1 line... 2 lines!! Never have I ever gotten 2 lines with a first response on any of my chemicals. They've only shown on the cheap tests.

I just couldn't believe it was real! I do know that I had been feeling rather dizzy most of the day. I'd also had an abundance of energy, like someone had stuck 2 Duracell batteries in me. And I literally couldn't stop peeing. It wasn't even funny anymore. I just sit down and then - boom - the pee fairy would hit me! Also, my hands had been freezing and they're never cold; and my nose was bunged up like I was getting a cold but my body was fine. I was also super, super horny to the point I wanted to rip the hubby's clothes off.

6DP 5DT: It was Mother's Day in the UK which was rather ironic considering we'd got our first official blazing positive. The words *Pregnant 1-2* were staring back at me. I felt so overwhelmed and joyous that words couldn't even come out of my mouth properly. I handed it to the hubby and just said, "I needed to pee so I did this, look!" He stared at it for a while, taking it all in, then leapt off his seat and gave me a huge hug saying the words, "Oh my god! Is this for real? Are we actually having a baby?"

Even though I was overwhelmed, my emotions were all over the place. I knew that the official test day was 5 days away so I didn't dare get excited. I felt like I was holding my breath. Going to bed that night after that result, I placed my hand on my belly and whispered, "I will protect you know matter what". That was when I felt the rush of love for something that would be no bigger than a grain of sand.

7DP 5DT: Getting out of bed at 5am to shove another Progesterone pessary up my foof, I just kept telling myself it was all worth it. That was until my alarm went off again and it was time to get up for work. Only, today I was going to work pregnant and nobody knew except the hubby of course! Working a 12-hour shift, I was exhausted halfway through. I literally had to have a nap and I was still feeling incredibly dizzy. I had to get up extra slowly to avoid nearly passing out. Hormones or progesterone? Who knows!

What also didn't help me out was that the clinic advise no sex within the 2 week wait but I felt like the blood had just rushed straight down to my fandango. It was now a craving. Crazy horny pregnant lady at your service! The hubby was being so good about it all and, as much as I begged, he said no. Part of me thanked him for this but the other part of me wanted to eat him alive! Only 4 more days until it was official test day and my tests were still getting darker by the day.

8DP 5DT: I woke up today with the mother of all headaches. I actually struggled to get out of bed because of it. I had a quick shower, splashing my face with cold water and giving the old lady cave a good scrub - those Progesterone tablets are messy as hell. They constantly made you feel like you'd peed yourself and the mess they left once they'd melted - yack! Climbing out of the shower, I felt somewhat refreshed and the headache had started to ease off.

Now I had to battle through a 12 hour shift, shattered, horny and hormonal. But I couldn't complain. I'd yearned to feel this way for years and now it was finally happening. And, once again, the tests were only getting stronger. I'd decided I was now a self-confessed pee on a stick addict. I just couldn't help myself. 3 more days until the official test day and that couldn't come quickly enough. The symptoms I'd been feeling so far were: dizziness when I stood up; craving for wholemeal toast and Liquorice Allsorts; tender, heavy boobs; tiredness mid-afternoon and a constantly bunged up nose.

9DP 5DT: My morning pee on a stick didn't happen this morning because in my sleepy state I completely forgot. The hubby was slightly gutted as he had woken up with me at 05:30, just to see the result change from day to day. I personally think it was rather sweet that he was so into it!

I woke up feeling rather sickly that morning. It didn't help either that the dog and the hubby decided to fart at the same time; my nose just couldn't handle it and I spent the next 5 minutes retching. Farts would be now banned in our house - unless they were mine because mine were like little unicorn puffs of rainbows that smelt like candy!

I got to work today, to do yet another 12-hour shift, and I was so tired. I needed some matchsticks! The hubby and I had also decided to tell our families and close friends the good news on Friday because that would be our official test day and, with the shit storm of the

Coronavirus happening around us right now, I would have to self-isolate so I think people would guess.

My symptoms of the day: I was still feeling tired but now I was starting to feel overwhelmed and emotional with it all; my boobs felt like giant boulders; I was still quite dizzy when I stood up from sitting, so I was having to get up slowly; I had low cramps but they weren't very strong - not as they were a couple of days ago.

10DP 5DT: There was just one more day until the official test day and the wait was killing me. I didn't think I would relax until I could ring the clinic with our result. Part of my brain thought that the test was just going to randomly turn negative. My brain was not functioning properly right now and everything seemed so unreal. Fecking hormones were getting to me, to the point where I couldn't even hold my tears in anymore. The other day I was crying because someone else's mam had died. I didn't even know them that well but that didn't stop my eyes streaming!

I peed on yet another stick and got the words *Pregnant 2-3*. I literally thought my eyes were deceiving me! I showed it to the hubby and he sat there mesmerised by the actual words. I couldn't wait until the next day when I could tell my mam and dad. I just wanted to tell them now! We'd gotten further in this pregnancy than in any of the chemicals so my mind had started to feel at ease and I was excited at the prospect that this was actually it!

My parents and brother were thrilled to bits. We had originally bought some scratch cards that revealed that we are pregnant but, upon handing them out, I totally forgot my parents needed glasses and couldn't even see the words! After fumbling for their glasses, they finally read out the words. My mam screeched with excitement and even my dad got a little bit emotional. He's very much like me in that he doesn't really show it so, when he does, I just know. My brother had been following our journey through IVF and was also overjoyed.

Leaving their house, we both felt such elation and joy. We'd never got to the stage of telling people as it had usually disappeared as quickly as it came. When we got home, we video called the hubby's family. Our niece's response was far the best as, when she was told the news, she burst into tears. So of course I then burst into tears - bloody hormones! It was such a shame to have to video call them all but, as the UK was currently on lockdown, I didn't think the police would deem it 'essential' for us to travel to Durham to let them all know. A party after all this shit storm was over was definitely on the cards!

By 11DP 5DT, it was OTD!! So our official test day had arrived and I woke up with excitement oozing out of me, praying that the hospitals' official pee stick would read positive just like all the others. Me and the hubby sat anxiously waiting for the pee to travel up the stick. Although we didn't have to wait long as it showed positive almost instantly! Jumping for joy, we realised that this was the end of our infertility journey. We were incredibly lucky that it had worked the first time with the IVF.

Next, I had to inform the clinic of our situation. Because, as much as I wanted to celebrate, with Covid19 hanging around like a bad smell, I simply didn't know what to do about going into work or anything! 9am came and I phoned the clinic hoping that nurse Jackie would be in. We couldn't wait to tell her the news but it wasn't Jackie who answered the phone. It was however the lovely admin lady Lorraine. This was someone, who every time we entered the clinic, asked how we were getting on and wished us luck. As I said the words to her on the phone, it dawned on me that it was the first time I'd said the words, "I'm pregnant". It felt so official and she was absolutely thrilled for us too.

She did get nurse Jackie to ring us back later. After the excitement and the congratulations had left the call, the seriousness started. The main issue being that, because Covid19 was still very much happening, I was to remain on lockdown for 12 weeks under the government guidelines! I would've gone back to work no bother but this virus was scaring the shit out of me. It didn't help either that the media scaremongered everyone about it with blatant lies!

So from today I would be on lockdown, only leaving the house to walk the dog down the street. This would be until April 17th - which would be our first official pregnancy scan date. This time they'd be looking for an actual baby and not just how many follicles were in my ovaries. We were still not out of the danger zone by far. We had 8 weeks to go until we were 'safe'. But until then, I would relax and enjoy every moment of this pregnancy, nausea and all.

Because - finally - I was very much pregnant!!!

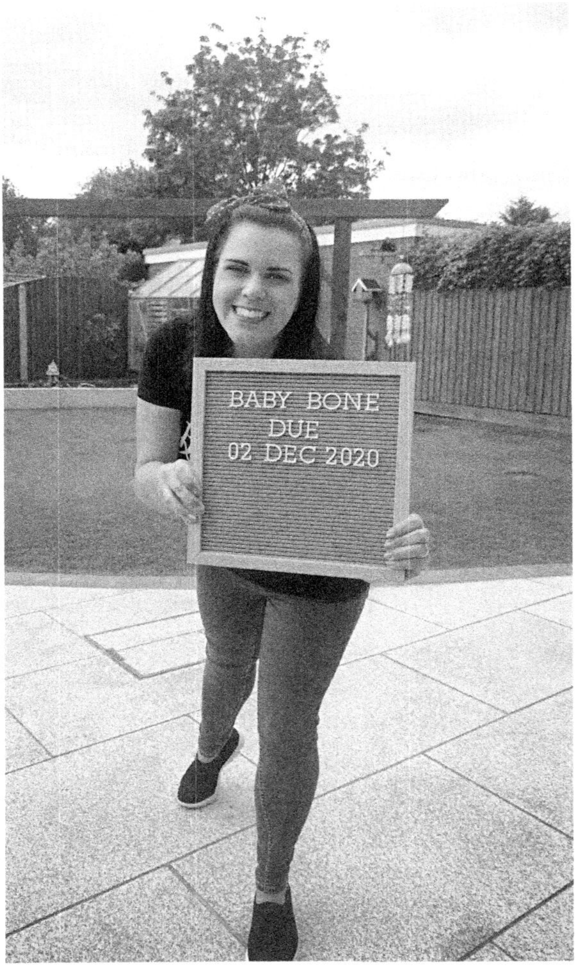
BABY BONE
DUE
02 DEC 2020

Printed in Great Britain
by Amazon